GRIEFSTRIKE!

McSWEENEY'S
SAN FRANCISCO

Copyright © 2022 Jason Roeder

All rights reserved, including right of reproduction
in whole or in part, in any form.

McSweeney's and colophon are registered trademarks of
McSweeney's, an independent publisher based in San Francisco.

Cover illustration by Benjamin Marra

Interior illustrations by Dale Cullinane

ISBN 978-1-952119-38-5

10 9 8 7 6 5 4 3 2 1

www.mcsweeneys.net

Printed in the United States

GRIEFSTRIKE!

The Ultimate Guide to Mourning

JASON ROEDER

McSWEENEY'S

SAN FRANCISCO

AUTHOR'S NOTE/DEDICATION

This book is a parody of a grief manual and of the kinds of issues we tend to confront when someone we love passes. If you find it legitimately insightful or comforting, I'm grateful, and I'll tell you in advance I have no earthly idea how I did that. But I do hope the book provides you with at least a funny moment or two in what's probably one of the more miserable stretches of your life. If for some reason you'd like an occasional glimpse into my actual experience, check out the Sincerity Corner asides which will pop up from time to time.

And if you're wondering who specifically inspired this book, it was my mother, Phyllis, who died in 2019. She loved her family and her cats and spent almost her entire professional life as a traveling home-health nurse, literally binding the wounds of the elderly. *Seeping* wounds. She had a car trunk full of gauze and catheters, and I would have lasted five full minutes at her job before cracking completely.

I know my mother would be proud of this book, partly because she thought I was funny but mostly because where her sons were concerned, she just couldn't help herself.

DEVASTATION PERFECTED

I didn't know your loved one. If I did, I probably would have liked them, and they would have liked me. Not *more* than they liked you, of course, but definitely *as* much. Because I have written a groundbreaking, paradigm-exploding therapeutic resource—if you want to grieve like a champion, like you're the Super Bowl MVP of your own sorrow, you've come to the right place. Sure, similar books exist, with squishy titles like *Cozy Words for Crying* or *A Casketful of Sunshine*, but this is the book your heart requires to truly, massively heal.

This is loss like a boss.

If you've made the mistake of reading those other books before this one, you've probably encountered morsels of so-called wisdom along the lines of: "Healing is rarely a straightforward process" or "It's unethical to leverage the death of your loved one into free teeth-whitening services." Ignore these experts. Their competence has blinded them to bold ideas. Their dependence on insights gleaned from years of intensive clinical experience has closed them off to newer and louder concepts. No, your recovery belongs in the hands of a man whose work is shelved alongside a coloring book for grown-ups and a compendium of Snoop Dogg haiku—therapeutic innovation, until it's properly recognized, is often dismissed as a novelty.

Other grief manuals are there to help if they can, tentatively submitting advice for your approval the way a gorilla tries out new words in sign language. *This* book is for everyone who has found themselves in a place of unfathomable sadness and thought, *If grief is a large hoop of fire, then where is my ramp and motorcycle?* In this dark chapter of your life, you want gigantic healing outcomes. And that's what you'll get. Just look at what this book guarantees, by the numbers:

38 percent more confidence you'll somehow make it out of this
48 percent less mind-body dilapidation
63 percent better graveside posture
Sobbing 18 percent less convulsive
49 percent more success keeping it together till you get to the parking lot
21 percent less wishing it were you
94 percent more wishing it was some stranger
50 percent less wondering what they're doing now, if anything
88 percent less likelihood of channeling anguish into artistic project for which you are not at all suited
52 percent less regret over eulogy that lacked certain pizzazz

These are just some of the results you can expect almost immediately from these pages. But what's *on* these pages that's going to get you there?

SUPERCHARGED HEALING

Before this book turns its full attention to grieving, chapter one provides a brief look at hospitals, those merry, sterile fortresses where sometimes doctors heal people and sometimes they say things like, "Sorry, but that pit bull really knew what it was doing." The next chapter dives into the aftermath, to the weeks and months you'll struggle to put your heart back together like a baby assembling an entertainment center, to the years you'll be mostly fine but never quite. What challenging feelings might you be experiencing, and how can you eliminate them with minimal time-consuming introspection?

If you've spent your life in loving relationships with family and friends, it's finally going to pay off in the discussion of getting the most from your support system. The chapter also explores how best to break the news to coworkers, social media acquaintances, and the Lyft driver who immediately regretted asking how you're doing this fine day. Of course, you'll ultimately have to do most of the emotional heavy lifting on your own, and the section on self-care will give you guidance on being kind to yourself, as well as diet and exercise tips especially designed to keep you piling on the muscle mass throughout your bereavement.

Once you've fortified your mind and body, you'll be ready for advice on keeping your loved one close in a way that's beautiful and meaningful but stops well short of wearing a fanny pack filled with hair clippings. Then, finally, you'll take the Informal Grief Archetype Assessment (IGAA). With the help of this self-diagnostic test which the American Psychological Association has hailed as "unfamiliar with" and "You're not using our logo, are you?" you'll understand how you grieve better than you ever dreamed you would as a child.

So now that you have a sense of what's inside this book, let's make absolutely sure you use it correctly.

PREPARING FOR THIS BOOK

While this book might seem magical, like something the grief-manual faeries might store in the hollow of an enchanted elm tree, it actually requires your full involvement. This can be challenging, I know. Your own inner turmoil, the assistance you're providing others, and the dark plans you're making for the cousin who no-showed the funeral have left you depleted. That's why I've developed five Grieving Visualization Power Postures which you can perform each time you pick up this book or any time you feel like you need that extra edge over your misery.

1. Driving Off as Your Grief Attempts to Board Your Bus

Begin standing nude in your sunroom. From there, gently squat as much as is comfortable to simulate being seated on the padded chair used by a municipal bus driver. Position your hands about a foot in front of your chest, as if gripping a steering wheel, and look straight ahead. Imagine your grief in your peripheral vision, slapping the door and waving around its stupid briefcase as you slowly and mercilessly pull into traffic.

2. Denying Your Grief Readmission to the Water Park

Begin standing nude in your sunroom. Your legs should be shoulder width apart. Swiftly extend one arm out to the side, as if you've noticed your grief attempting to reenter Splashtown. Picture yourself refusing to budge as your grief explains that it just ran out to the car for a second. Feel free to repeat the words, "No hand stamp, no reentry," over and over, and imagine your grief muttering, "Fucking asshole," as it tries to get its wife on the phone.

3. Shutting Down the Deli That Has Been in Grief's Family for Three Generations

Begin standing nude in your sunroom. Now, reach out and smooth into place the large decal declaring that Grief's New York Style Delicatessen is hereby closed by order of the commissioner of health and mental hygiene. Show no expression as you imagine

grief sobbing that no restaurant ever recovers from this kind of black mark and that you're flushing its whole damn livelihood straight down the toilet. Optionally, you might smirk just a touch when your grief whimpers, "I hope you're happy."

4. Notifying Your Grief That It Actually Didn't Get into Princeton on the Day of Its Congratulatory Celebration

Begin standing nude in your sunroom. Hold one hand next to your face, as if talking on the telephone. Relish the concern seeping into your grief's face when you announce that you're from the office of admissions, that you're sorry to report it received an acceptance letter in error, and that, no, it wasn't even waitlisted. Savor the moment when it shushes the friends and family enjoying themselves in the background and the sudden muting of a party playlist. Say aloud the words, "You know, community colleges are actually a far better option than most people realize," and then gently lower the hand holding the receiver, imagining your grief screaming at its parents to just get rid of the stupid cake—which says, "You Did It, Grief!"—before it literally throws up.

5. Abandoning Your Grief on the Moon

Begin standing nude in your sunroom. Vigorously skip in place, as if bounding across the low-gravity lunar surface. After a few moments, pause at the entrance to your lander and turn your gaze to where your grief is obliviously collecting rock samples a few hundred feet away. Now, march in place and grasp rungs in the air, as if climbing a ladder into the

rocket, then give your grief a thumbs-up as you blast off and leave it on the moon's barren surface with about three hours of oxygen in its suit.

You are now ready for Chapter 1.

A Short History of Grief

Strange as it may seem, there is some debate as to when the intense sadness characterizing grief actually began. Some historians point out that the ancient Greeks, for example, dispassionately marked the passing of a loved one with a phrase like, *Tóra zoun sto chomátino diamérisma*, which roughly translates into, "Now they live in the dirt apartment." Millennia prior, the Egyptians blandly depicted the experience of losing a loved one with a hieroglyph of a cobra ignoring a corpse pile. And, of course, as recently as the mid-nineteenth century, Abraham Lincoln famously said of the thousands of young soldiers killed at Gettysburg, "We acknowledge these brave men yet in truth feel nothing."

To this day, no one knows how exactly grief came into being. Was it a germ, a powerful genetic mutation, an obscure zoning ordinance that has devastatingly somehow remained on the books? What we do know for absolute certain is that, by the turn of the twentieth century, documentary evidence of grief had emerged, even if it still wasn't quite understood by those experiencing it. Upon the death of her longtime husband, for example, one Austrian baroness wrote in her journal: "His passing seems to have produced a peculiar sense of unease, as if something within me has actually died as well. That makes no sense, of course. Instead, I shall have the kitchen staff hanged at once in the *Heldenplatz* for serving me rancid meats."

Grief Journal Prompts

1. Write down your favorite memory of your loved one. Then, write down all remaining memories of your loved one, followed by all unrelated memories until you have completely duplicated your mind on paper.

2. Complete this sentence using as many words as you'd like: "Using only a compass, twine, and a pocketknife, I will be compassionate to myself by _____."

3. Is this a photo of your loved one? If so, write about how it makes you feel. If your loved one is not former *Law & Order* star Jerry Orbach, paste a second photo next to the provided one and freewrite for ten minutes about how the two together make you feel.

4. Fill in the blanks: "When I think of my loved one, I feel _____ inside. If I could tell him or her anything, it would be _____ _____ _____, which actually isn't at all uncommon for an aroused swan."

CHAPTER I

HOSPITALS: PREGAMING FOR GRIEF

If life is what happens when you're making other plans, death is what happens when those plans get postponed for all eternity. We all die and it's forever, no matter what our cryosleep sales consultant tells us. So far, death is undefeated by humanity, and let me be the first to tell you that you're not going to be the person who pulls off the upset. Sometimes death is sudden, maybe precipitated by an eerily innocuous remark, such as "I can't even fathom getting assassinated in a place like Dallas" or "I'm axe-proof." But death often announces that it will be swinging by the neighborhood sometime in the near or intermediate future—a terminal diagnosis, a slow but unmistakable deterioration, a crow suddenly appearing on the windowsill dressed as an undertaker. We think of grief as the bad feeling that's brought about by the bad event, but grief can actually begin in anticipation of the death to come. You're bracing yourself, letting go a little, even as you're still hoping for some medical or divine or, at this point, alien intervention. It's the toughest balance to strike, and you're attempting to do it when you're as exhausted as you've ever been, like you should have some top-secret government clearance to even access that kind of fatigue. And all of this in the place singularly dedicated to reminding us of our mortality and the many splendid ways we can breathe our last breath: a hospital.

A HOSPITAL WHO'S WHO

Of course, lots of miraculous procedures take place in hospitals—organs are transplanted, conjoined twins are separated as surely as a strongman rips a phonebook in half, and a bullet is removed from the face of someone who will thankfully live to improperly clean a rifle another day. But as time goes on, it may come to pass that your loved one is in residence for a while, and that cannot possibly be a great development. You may end up spending a good deal of time at the hospital yourself, trying to be helpful and sometimes succeeding but mostly being an obstacle a nurse has to get around to change an IV. Pass enough days and weeks at a hospital, and you'll likely end up spending time with a particular cast of characters:

The Coworker You Weren't Expecting, but OK

Funny, your dad never even mentioned this guy. Or maybe he did once. Hard to say. He's here visiting now in any case. That's nice. A little weird, but nice. Dennis, was it?

The Luscious but Poorly Timed Medical Professional

You're just trying to keep vigil when along comes this doctor or nurse who's making you feel things you did not expect to feel in the same room where your loved one's oxygen is being intensely monitored. It's intrusive sexiness like this that makes you wonder if our broken healthcare system can ever truly be repaired.

The Mysterious Patient Next Door

You can't help but peek in her room on your way to your loved one's room. Who is she? How sick is she? That young man with her, probably her son. And someone brought her balloons. That's nice. But they're starting to crinkle, a bit at odds with their "Get Well Soon!" messaging, don't you think? And then one day she's gone. That's good news, right? Of course it is. You just saw her eating soup yesterday, totally unassisted no less. Yep, she's great. She's home and well and great.

The Wonderful but Out-Of-Network Cardiologist
She was the best, so naturally she's not covered by insurance. Wonder what sort of asshole we'll get stuck with instead.

The Acquaintance Who Overstays Her Already Limited Welcome
The facts are these. Your mother was in a book club for six months. Charlotte was in that club for three of them but has nevertheless been taking up a chair in her intermediate care room all morning. Even a purely performative invitation to grab lunch in the cafeteria has failed to dislodge her. The sun's going down when she eventually leaves, and you remember your mom telling you the book club came to a halt whenever that idiot opened her mouth.

The Kidney Doctor Who Doesn't Want to Hear About Other Body Parts
This gentleman is a nephrologist. Look it up, asshole. Kidneys are his lifelong specialty, and there's literally nothing he cares less about in this world than the interconnectivity of organ systems. Even say the words "lungs" or "intestines" in his presence and watch his body tense up, as if daring you to say it again, just once.

The Estranged Relative Who's Here to Make Nice
Well, well, well, look who abandoned her brother for no reason a full decade ago and just showed up to take advantage of someone who's probably more forgiving on painkillers.

The Ghost of the Internist
You've never actually seen him, the doctor coordinating your loved one's treatment, but you've sensed him. A cold spot in the hallway, a barely perceptible rattle in the clipboard in the rack outside the room.

You ask at the front desk where he is and when he'll be back, and they'll tell you the only person by that name died a hundred years ago. Or might be doing rounds at another hospital, no one's exactly sure.

HEALTH CARE DIRECTIVES

When we're admitted to a hospital, we have certain expectations about the treatment we'll receive. For example, if we're bleeding profusely, we assume a qualified medical professional will stanch the flow and not post photos online of the real gusher they've got in room 204. We trust that if we swallow our tongue, someone's going to stop by and nail that rascal to the bottom of our mouth. And, of course, if our heart stops, every doctor and nurse on the floor is going to drop whatever they're doing and dramatically punch it back to life—no one is dying on their watch, except possibly the patients they left behind in the other rooms.

But it's not always so simple. When someone is already terminally ill, for example, they may want to forgo certain heavy-duty interventions. Or, if they're not capable of making those decisions, a family member or other proxy may be forced to do so. That lucky so-and-so could be you, so it's a good idea to be broadly acquainted with some of the available options.

Full Code. Doctors and nurses take any measures known to medical science—medications, chest compressions, a breathing tube hooked up to a ventilator—before desperately turning to other fields, such as carpentry and controlled demolition. It's the default starting point until your loved one (or you, on their behalf) opts out of one or more aspects of treatment.

Do Not Resuscitate (DNR). Under this order, CPR will not be

Know Your Hospital Televisions

You're stuck all day in a hospital room. The Internet connection is spotty, and you'd feel weird about using public Wi-Fi to sell your rhino horn sex elixir on the dark web anyway. You brought a book, but you're just too fuzzy right now to take on a heavy lift like Rob Lowe's memoir. Your only option for some much-needed distraction is the sweet oblivion cube mounted on the ceiling above you. But not all hospital room TVs are created equal.

Tier 1: Mostly functional basic cable with kind of a hazy wobble here and there.

Tier 2: Buttons on the bedside remote only work to increase the volume, not decrease it. Vast expanses of empty blue screens, although main channels are intact once you find them.

Tier 3: Red bulb on remote control lights up, but nothing happens. You have to drag over a small stool absolutely not meant to be stood upon to change channels manually. Most of the channels are like staticky transmissions from outer space, but you know they're not because you catch a glimpse of two seniors in a tandem kayak from a Lipitor commercial.

Tier 4: Nothing's operational, and, yes, it's plugged in. The nurse doesn't know what the deal is and seems very close to telling you it's not her job to hook you up with *Judge Mathis*.

Tier 5: The television not only doesn't work, but every attempt to operate it breaks another television in the hospital. Press the "on" button long enough, and you will eventually break every television in the world.

Tier 6: TV's fine. You just feel guilty watching it.*

---

* **Sincerity Corner:** Because anything less than the most nonstop, determined concentration on my intubated mother felt like an act of neglect. Even holding her hand or talking to her felt stupidly incomplete. Ultimately, there's so much waiting, so much sheer sitting there, that watching a few minutes of whatever Channel 5 was serving up at three in the afternoon was a perfect way to just park my attention for a few minutes.

performed, no matter how tantalizingly compressible the chest looks.

Do Not Intubate (DNI). Sometimes paired with a DNR, this prohibits use of a breathing tube. In most states, however, doctors may still insert a breathing tube for aesthetic reasons, such as the way the tube draws attention away from neck fat. Note that neither the patient nor their representative can prevent this form of beautifying procedure.

Resuscitate but Don't Go Crazy (RBDGC). Under this order, CPR *is* indicated, but nobody needs to knock themselves out. Seriously, it's nice that so many people want to help, but if thirty seconds isn't getting it done, it's OK to call it a day.

Intubate a Stranger (IAS). The IAS builds upon the DNI by stipulating that, while you don't want your loved one to receive a breathing tube, you do want a person at random to receive one. Exceedingly rare and a subject of heated ethical debate due to the unproven medical value of snatching someone off the street and connecting their lungs to a machine for no real reason.

Wait Until Birthday to Resuscitate (WUBTR). This order delays attempts at life-saving CPR until that most special day of the year rolls around. It's true that without CPR, a person is typically braindead in a matter of minutes, but just think how fun it'd be if you held out for another seven months and nine days.

Resuscitate Only If a Basset Hound Does It (ROIABHDI). Authorizes resuscitation only on the condition that a basset hound, preferably with a tiny lab coat and its long ears adorably flopping over the tubes of a toy stethoscope, revives the heart using its stumpy but surprisingly powerful legs. The specificity is important, as hospitals have faced litigation from patients who were brought back but horrified to discover a dachshund had been responsible.

MILKING THE INEVITABLE FOR ALL IT'S WORTH: HOSPICE CARE

In less fortunate places or eras, death is pretty much always in attendance. You emerge from the womb, and there's already half a dozen forms of lethal diarrhea waiting to say hello. If you somehow linger to age thirty, people come from hundreds of miles around to gawk at your single gray eyebrow hair. Most of us in America don't have that kind of relationship with death. We're too busy forging our destinies and telling ourselves we can be anything we set our minds to being, no matter how much logic begs us to accept the limitations of our strength, intelligence, or ability to sexually perform in front of a camera crew. Then someone we love gets sick, so sick that there's no motivating it away. They're still with us for now, but they're going, even though we read some inspirational story on the Internet about how someone with a very similar condition survived and went on to heroically climb Mt. Everest (eight Sherpas carrying his luggage were killed). But this is not that story, unfortunately. In this story, modern medicine is plumb out of ideas. There's expected to be six months or less and an opportunity to make the most of the worst, otherwise known as hospice.

You've probably already noticed that the first five letters of "hospital," "hospice," and even "hospitality" are the same. That's because they share the same Latin root, *hospitium*, meaning "inn where sickly travelers expire in their sleep." Hospice isn't mandatory, of course. Doctors are going to keep attempting treatment by default, though by this point they've determined a real fix is not in the cards. But once someone's in hospice, there's no obligation to remain there—if researchers suddenly discovered chowder cured cancer, no one would deny your loved one a piping-hot bread bowl.

Assume, however, that he or she has been transitioned from hospital to hospice and is going to stay there for the duration. What does that mean?

It's really about cure vs. comfort. In hospice, you're conceding that, well, yes, barring an absolutely stupid miracle, your loved one is going to die. But in exchange, a team of doctors, nurses, therapists, and even a clergy member if your loved one goes in for that sort of fun, can help them manage pain, symptoms, and emotional distress, allowing them to pass on in dignity and relative comfort. While there are independent hospice centers and hospice wings in hospitals, many people elect for their hospice care to take place at home where they can relax in their favorite chair, get some snuggle time in with their dog,* or enjoy one last Halloween of spraying weed killer on trick-or-treaters.

Eventually, however, the end is nigh. Not just nigh, but very, very nigh.

LAST WORDS THAT WOW

If human history has taught us one thing, it's that people will die pretty much anywhere, though it's not a bad bet that the last words you share with your loved one will be in a hospital or hospice. Of course, there's

---

* **Sincerity Corner:** My mother wasn't in the hospital's in-house hospice wing very long. She was given a day or two at most, but more likely hours. We asked if we could bring her cat, an absolutely gargantuan orange tabby named Peaches, to her room. They said yes unexpectedly, sparing us the calculations of smuggling an eighteen-pound animal in a squirming backpack. I wish I could say her eyes lit up when I placed my mother's hand on the cat's fur, but she was really struggling by that point. I'm choosing to focus on the possibility that she could feel him purr.

no guarantee that you'll be there when the fateful moment arrives. Even if you're sticking close to the adjustable bed you're now absolutely certain your loved one will not be getting up from, you still might miss the moment they pass just by ducking out to grab a little fresh air or get a wicked-looking hellhound airbrushed on your car. And if you're not there, you might not even remember what your last conversation turned out to be. Or you do, but it's something about when the food service worker will be back with another fruit cup.

This is all to say that if you're fortunate enough to be there—"fortunate" as in having the opportunity to say goodbye on your own terms, not that the experience itself will be some sort of cruise ship tequila tasting—you need to be ready for that all-important moment because you'll only have one chance to say what needs to be said.

First, seize the initiative. If they sense they're down to their last few minutes, your loved one might want to leave you with a final message of love, encouragement, or even bittersweet regret. It may be something they've been meaning to tell you for a very long time. Just go ahead and gently cut them off mid-sentence. You've got something prepared, and the longer they go on, the more likely you are to forget it. They can always pick up right where they left off if they're still around after you've said all you have to say.

Now that you've taken the wheel, it's essential you get where you're going quickly. Pare down unnecessary preamble, such as "I recall a fascinating article *The Atlantic* did on this very topic..." or "Set phasers for fun!" In fact, you might want to have a few key objectives in mind that you can use as guideposts along the way. They'll vary from person to person, but they could proceed sort of like these:

1. Succinct introduction.

2. Declaration of affection/devotion.

3. Apology for occasions where you've wronged loved one over course of life. (Omit if others have always been to blame.)

4. Small, tender joke.

5. Reiteration of love.

6. Optional call to action (social media, website, podcast, etc.).

7. Final goodbye.

Also, be sure to focus on the specific language you're using. When someone doesn't have much time left, it's a real shame to put them to sleep for the duration. Here's where impact words come into play. Consider these statements from two daughters:

"I'll miss you, and I'm so proud to be your daughter. I love you."

Adequate, sure. Even heartfelt. But dynamic? A goodbye that's going to move the needle? Hardly. But her sister is going to give that same sentiment some energy and authority:

"Over four-plus superlative decades as your daughter, I have cultivated the most robust feelings of emotional attachment toward you, consistently setting new industry-leading standards in affection."

Now imagine it's you drawing your last breaths, hearing from your two daughters. Which one seems like the simple child you don't necessarily regret having but might keep a little distance from when she joins you in the afterlife? And which one seems like a go-getter, an enterprising asset to any deathbed? Which would *you* want to be?

Finally, remember that what you don't say can be as important as what you do say. If you're struggling to find the right words, you can't go wrong by holding your loved one's hand or gently blowing into a conch. Or just sitting quietly. What matters is that you're there, and you *didn't* blurt out the fact that you'll actually be burying them deep in the woods because you already squandered the money for their cemetery plot on unlicensed Marvel-branded crypto called HulkToken. There is profound love in that silence.

Using a Last Word Service

If you're absolutely certain that you're going to blow it, that you'll say something so hideous you'll spend the rest of your life hoping God was too busy inventing new birth defects to have overheard, you might consider a last word service. Companies such as ByeBuddy and Grim Speaker will dispatch a courier to your loved one's bedside and deliver customized parting remarks according to your specific instructions. While the services can be pricey—upward of ten thousand dollars per visit unless a tragically discounted family package is purchased—the applications are surprisingly short, such as the one for FlatLines below.

1. **Subject to availability, what sort of messenger should we send?**
   (a) Rough approximation of you which won't be detected due to your loved one's cataracts
   (b) Drone with mounted megaphone
   (c) Pizza delivery person who could use a few extra bucks
   (d) Former inmate who wants to be part of the solution for once

2. How long would you like your messenger to interact with your loved one?
   (a) Thirty minutes
   (b) Twenty minutes
   (c) Ten minutes
   (d) Thirty-second Adios Express special

3. What is your preferred emotional tenor?
   (a) Shattered
   (b) Wistful
   (c) Wrathful
   (d) Stoic as befits rigid military upbringing
   (e) A tantalizing *je ne sais quoi*

4. How religious should the message be?
   (a) Drearily atheist
   (b) Observant, but nothing too exhausting
   (c) Orthodox lite
   (d) May only be delivered by circumcised male or male willing to be circumcised on the spot

5. Which of the following statements that you've never been able to bring yourself to say would you like your messenger to declare during their visit?
   (a) "I love you."
   (b) "I'm proud of you."
   (c) "It was me who ratted you out to the ecoterrorism division of the FBI."
   (d) "I know you intentionally raised me genderless so I could choose myself one day, but could you please go ahead and pick one because I'm forty-two and still haven't decided."

Grief Journal Prompts

1. If there was a doctor or nurse who provided excellent care for your loved one in the hospital, write their name here so that you can send them a thank-you card; if not, just write "Neglected." _____

2. Who were you most grateful to have visit your loved one in the hospital? Who was a nuisance? Write down the ways their presence may have hindered your loved one's recovery.

3. Would you characterize your overall hospital experience as a good one? If not, devise an alternative system for carrying out quality medical care on a national scale in the blank provided: _____.

4. If you've said goodbye to your loved one, write down your last words to them as best as you can recall so you'll never have to worry about forgetting them. "_____ _____ _____ _____ , allowing me to triple your initial five hundred thousand dollar investment in just twelve months, despite the fact that most countries have banned commercial whaling and _____ _____ _____."

CHAPTER II

FUN WITH AFTERMATH

It happened. Death, that is. You knew it would happen but somehow never thought it would. Death was *over there*. It was the reason visits to Grandma stopped in a hurry and what happened when Mario mistimed a fireball jump and the rationale for mummies. But now, and maybe quite abruptly, it's as close as a hospital bed or whatever they could find in the belly of that jaguar. You want to process it, and you're absolutely terrified of the proposition. You don't even know if you're numb or emotionally overheating—can you somehow be both? And maybe death isn't so close after all. Maybe it's still *over there*. But now you're over there too, looking back on who you were and fear you won't exactly be again. In this state, a nice man at the funeral home lets you know your loved one can be buried with a lagoon view for around twenty-five thousand dollars more.*

So what do you do now, when the last thing you probably want to do is anything? It can seem as if the various arrangements you suddenly have to make and your need to grieve are wrenching you in two equally painful directions. People often say they feel like a tug-of-war rope yanked from opposite sides at a summer camp for mastodons. The good news is that you can get through it. But it's rough right out of the gate.

---

* **Sincerity Corner:** In the movies, funerals just materialize onscreen with people attending them. In reality, there was an honest-to-God PowerPoint presentation at the funeral home where we could choose the material for the casket and the ornamentation we wanted, ranging from plain to essentially an Elvis jumpsuit. And there was indeed a pricey lagoon view option, which my mother never would've forgiven us for. Instead, she has a shady spot near a bench, as well as a view *of* the lagoon view and all the chumps who wasted a ton of cash.

FUNERALS: LET'S GET THIS
PARTY STARTED SOLEMNLY

There's nothing quite like standing in the same room as your deceased loved one to put in perspective that infamous potluck where your coleslaw brought a rare intestinal parasite back from the brink of extinction. It's a nasty time, generally speaking, and you have every right to be inconsolable, to feel however you're going to feel. If all you want is for this miserable production to be over so you can get yourself home, lie on the floor, and let despair pulsate through your body for an hour or all eternity, that's a fine thing to feel.

But a funeral can also be an occasion for healing. No, not a miracle where your loved one pops out of the casket alive and holding a bowl of your favorite soup in each hand, but a moment to celebrate their life and discover, maybe for the first time, how they affected others. When there are no more new memories to be made with you, the memories of those people—the coworker who'll miss your loved one's dedication to their job, the old friend reminiscing about childhood pranks, the army buddy with tales of heroic deeds and nothing at all happening in that village—can keep your loved one alive just a little longer and in ways you didn't expect.

What kind of funeral, though? Well, if your loved one went ahead and prearranged it, you just have to show up at the appointed hour without a distracting hygiene concern. If not, and if the responsibility did not fall to an infinitely more reliable sibling, you've got a few options:

Traditional Funeral
Timeless and classic. Truly a funeral's funeral that gets your loved one out of the chapel and into the earth with standard dignity.

Surefire Eulogy Starters

The hardest part of any written composition is getting it off the ground. But you're well on your way once you do. That's why it took Charles Dickens two decades to write the words, "It was the best of times, it was the worst of times," but also why he finished the rest of A *Tale of Two Cities* in five minutes, between bites of a muffin. So, if you're stuck on your eulogy and would very much like to avoid alienating a bunch of devastated people in a chapel, use one of these openers to give your send-off some liftoff.

"I'm going to keep this short, as my mother always said my speaking voice was a source of humiliation and sorrow."

"More than anything, my uncle would've wanted me to read off the names of apps I have on my phone and then immediately sit down."

"When words fail us, it only means it is time for improvised puppetry to begin."

"Forgive my brevity, but public speaking makes my guts absolutely erupt."

"What can I say at this moment that C+C Music Factory didn't say better thirty years ago?"

"I'm not wrong for wearing a belly shirt. You're wrong for staring."

"Who here remembers where they were for the finale of *Survivor: Cambodia?*"

"Now's as good a time as any to see how many ribs I can eat in five minutes."

"I take comfort in knowing my cousin will be spared the approaching environmental cataclysm."

"Hang on to your jockstraps!"

"Given the time crunch, I think we'll proceed straight to the Q&A."

PRO: Most funeral homes can crank one of these out with five minutes' notice; good starter funeral for families new to death and looking for a "no muss, no fuss" send-off.

CON: Not all that original. Few mourners will report service really blew tits to kingdom come.

Memorial Service

Like a traditional funeral, except the body is not present because it has already been interred or detonated and divvied up among organ recipients.

PRO: One less dead person in room; mourners can snack without eerie sense they're being watched.

CON: Eulogies must be shouted or spoken through megaphone so loved one can hear from grave in cemetery thousand feet away.

"Fun" Funeral

For the person who said they didn't want anyone to be sad at their funeral and actually meant it.

PRO: Smiles, laughter, kissing booth.

CON: Persistent pangs of blasphemy; awkwardness of having to nudge casket aside to find outlet for bubble machine.

Eco-Friendly Funeral

A service for those who want to be remembered first and foremost as biodegradable.

PRO: Minimal impact on Earth; embalming fluids not used for body but may be brought home to-go by next of kin.

CON: Slightly less elaborate observance than one you once had for pet hamster.

Home Funeral
Affordable DIY alternative in which family takes temporary custody of deceased until the body is buried, cremated, or adopted and brought into forever home.
PRO: More intimate way to experience death; great way to meet neighbors you've been meaning to have over.
CON: Going forward, hard to see TV room as anything else but place you bathed dead aunt.

CASKETS: MORTALITY'S CONTAINER STORE

The first coffins are believed to have originated in ancient China, supposedly as decorative packaging for a god of death who loved unwrapping gifts even though he always knew he'd just be getting another corpse. These days, it seems like there are as many casket designs as there are ways to die in the first place. Burial is a business like anything else, after all, and a conscientious funeral counselor will help you find the right bon voyage box at the right price. But beware the upsell. Don't let yourself be taken advantage of by someone offering useless frills like these:

Side-Sleeper Pillow. It's understood that your loved one will be resting on his or her back for eternity, so special, ergonomically contoured cushions aren't necessary.

Grave Robber Peephole. Fear is a common sales tactic, so don't be surprised if you get the hard sell for a tiny opening your loved one can peer through to help them determine if the person who's dug them up is a friend exhuming them just to say hello or someone with more sinister motives.

Coffin Lid Extension Leaf. Don't listen when an unscrupulous funeral counselor tells you the casket should have an extra panel that can be inserted into the lid in case your loved one has company over and needs room for everyone to sit.

Elastic Waistband: Remember, your loved one isn't exactly going to be packing on the pounds, so don't get talked into a coffin that promises to expand with any body shape.

Lawn Mower Bag. Don't let yourself get talked into this wholly unnecessary accessory for collecting grass trimmings. Mulching blades are generally legitimate, however.

HEADSTONES: HELLO, MY NAME WAS

We all know how important a first impression is. Sometimes that's the difference between landing that big job or being dragged out of the interview by security and sold to an underground circus. But we don't consider last impressions very much, specifically the ones engraved on our headstones. And that's a shame because it's the statement we'll make over and over until archaeologists fifty thousand years from now dig us up in hopes that our jawbones are interesting. In fact, there's a reasonable chance your loved one passed without leaving instructions for how they want to be memorialized on their headstone, leaving it to you to find those perfect words.

No need to rush. The words you want may not come to you immediately, and that's OK. A cemetery will often provide a simple, temporary marker like a small placard or a scarecrow, so take the time you need to craft your inscription. Remember, these are the all-important words which you will look upon every time you visit and that a groundskeeper will wave a leaf blower over twice a week—however long it takes to get it right is the appropriate amount of time.

Brevity is key. You don't have a lot of room to work with, so you can skip extraneous greetings and signoffs like "Dear Headstone" and "Sent from my Samsung Galaxy."

Be original but not too original. Individuality is as American as loaded potato skins or letting a virus burn through a population pretty much unchecked, and a headstone engraving is no exception. But while a bit of originality can make your loved one's headstone stand out gloriously in a giant field of dead people who couldn't care less, too much can literally set in stone something wacky or bizarre that won't stand the test of time. Even if you're the final decision-maker, be sure to run your ideas by others who were also close to your loved one. The last thing you want is for a vandal to spray-paint a penis on the headstone primarily out of pity.

Paint a picture with lettering. While a headstone will occasionally have a small, mounted portrait to remind visitors that the deceased once looked way, way better than they do right now, it usually relies on lettering for its visual impact. And that comes down to selecting the right font:

Serif. Basic and readable. Perfect if you want a heartfelt inscription worthy of a newspaper's coverage of the UN climate summit.

Sans serif. More modern than serif fonts, and a cleaner look that subtly yet undeniably evokes the Target logo.

Calligraphy. Flowing and elegant, calligraphy is a sophisticated choice that says, "Something absolutely *enchanting* is happening in this casket, and don't you wish you were invited!"

Gothic. The preferred option if your loved one was accursed and died only after villagers buried his or her heart in the consecrated ground of a churchyard.

Alternating. With this budget-conscious option, you can cut the cost of the headstone engraving in half by inscribing only every other letter and counting on visitors to figure out pretty much what you're getting at.

Spelled Out in Shrimp and Mackerel. The only option in many seafaring communities, even the most landlocked among us can still have our passion for trawl fishing commemorated for all eternity.

EXPERIENCING GRIEF:
SADNESS HAS BEEN WORKING OUT

Maybe while you were scrambling to get your hands on funeral attire*— because the only appropriate item of clothing you owned were the black slacks you wore in 2003 to seat guests at a Steak and Ale—you were too distracted to truly contemplate the small matter of your emotional wreckage. But now, the funeral is over, the well-wishers have gone home, and you're trying to decide what to do at the moment, and possibly for the rest of your life. The pain is so gigantic, you have no idea how it's all fitting inside you, and all your usual coping strategies are flopping so, so badly. Nothing prepared you for this, and really, what was going to? Your goth phase did not deliver.

And yet, there's a path through—or a great many paths, depending on how much time you want to spend googling "help with unen-durable sadness" or, if you're on a budget, "coupon code for help

---

* **Sincerity Corner:** I know how crazily counterintuitive this seems, but I did not want to spend any time at Men's Wearhouse the week of my mother's funeral. However, at that unreal moment, it was actually a useful distraction that, for an hour or so any-way, grounded me in the stupid, familiar world again.

with unendurable sadness." One of the better-known models for this process was devised in 1969 by Swiss psychologist Elisabeth Kübler-Ross, her five stages of grief.

1. Denial. You might be familiar with this in terms of the quality of your screenplay or your conviction that she's coming back to you after twelve years of returning your letters unopened but with knife punctures. It's the wall you immediately put up between you and the unthinkable situation.

Typical thoughts:

"This isn't happening."

"When Dad gets back, we're going to sue the funeral home for putting him through that stressful cremation."

2. Anger. The intensity of this moment has arrived, and here's where you lash out at anyone and anything that made you feel this terrible way—doctors, family members, even your loved one themself for believing you when you said there was no risk in taking a chartered helicopter ride with a pilot whose license was revoked twenty years ago and was originally issued by Jimmy John's to begin with.

Typical thoughts:

"Fuck this. Fuck everything."

"I'm going to destroy this miserable world and every other planet just in case they were thinking of making a move against me."

How Much Am I Allowed to Blame God?
A State-By-State Breakdown

You've no doubt heard the saying, "Death is just the parfait station at the end of the buffet line we call life." But you just might not be in the mood to accept that death is part of life. You're angry deep down and demand to know who's responsible. Sometimes that's as easy as recalling the naughty thing that cocaine made the ride operator do. Often, however, there's no real culprit, no one suspect you can point at in a lineup and say, "Him. That's the man who caused bone cancer."

But then there's God. It's only natural to want to blame Him. After all, death—whether lingering or sudden, deadly microbe or three-way submarine collision—was His innovation. And there's no real divine risk in blaming Him since He tends to punish people at random anyway. But can you *legally*? Are there limits to how often you can climb your tallest ladder and try to spit on Heaven? Well, in this country, a lot actually depends on the state you live in.

State	Can I Legally Blame God For My Loved One's Death?
Alabama	No.
Alaska	Yes. Licensed residents may also track and hunt the Almighty.
Arizona	No. Except for deaths specifically caused by God's creations, e.g. coordinated scorpion ambush.
Arkansas	No.
California	Yes. Partially subsidized by state.
Colorado	Yes.
Connecticut	Yes.
Delaware	Yes. Additionally, many out-of-state residents use Delaware's business-friendly laws to lash out at God anonymously through an LLC.
Florida	Undetermined. While laws currently exist that forbid Florida residents from blaming God for making them strip naked and rob a convenience store with a spray nozzle hose attachment, it's unclear if those restrictions would be applied in the case of a loved one's death.
Georgia	Yes. But then you better run.

Hawaii	Yes.
Idaho	No.
Illinois	Yes. Chicago and certain suburbs only.
Indiana	No. God actually given option of blaming you.
Iowa	No.
Kansas	No.
Kentucky	Yes. But only non-Judeo-Christian deities.
Louisiana	No.
Maine	Yes.
Maryland	Yes.
Massachusetts	Fuck yeah, you'll love it.
Michigan	Yes.
Minnesota	Yes. But why would you go and do a thing like that?
Mississippi	No. Also extradites fugitives who blamed God in state of origin.
Missouri	No.
Montana	No.
Nebraska	No. God may only be blamed for pests, such as leaf beetles and cloverworms, causing poor soybean harvests.
Nevada	No. God draws millions of tourists to the state each year with His cabaret residency at Zappos Theater at Planet Hollywood Resort & Casino.
New Hampshire	Yes.
New Jersey	Yes.
New Mexico	Yes.
New York	Yes. Many residents, however, drive down to New Jersey where blaming God is a bit less expensive.
North Carolina	No.
North Dakota	No. Residents required to thank God in writing for inviting loved one to paradise.
Ohio	Yes.
Oklahoma	No.
Oregon	Yes. As well as for deaths of nonhuman animals and glaciers.
Pennsylvania	Yes.
Rhode Island	Yes.
South Carolina	No. "God Takes What's His" is literally state motto.

South Dakota	No.
Tennessee	No.
Texas	No. In fact, law banning blaming God for loved one's death is only law in entire state.
Utah	No. Penalty for violations $1,000 fine and up to six weeks on sex offender registry.
Vermont	Yes.
Virginia	Yes.
Washington	Yes. Up to 40 percent of blame may be laid at feet of supreme being statewide. (Seattle residents, however, are automatically registered to blame God and must opt out in person at City Hall.)
West Virginia	No.
Wisconsin	Yes.
Wyoming	Yes. But very restrictive, only kicking in after death of third immediate family member within six-month timeframe.

3. Bargaining. In the case of someone still in the process of dying, this is your attempt to cut a deal with death, who, as of the writing of this book, has never once negotiated. For example, if your loved one is spared, you'll stop drinking or at least minimize the frequency with which you wake up in a stranger's attic wearing a second stranger's hairpiece. When your loved one has already passed, bargaining can still take place, but it's in the form of a what-if mental exercise, sometimes tinged with guilt or remorse.

Typical thoughts:

"This wouldn't have happened if I were a better son."

"If I hadn't selfishly volunteered to cleanse the bedsores of paraplegic veterans, I might've been home to call an ambulance."

4. Depression. It's dawning on you, in all its overabundant grossness and injustice, that someone important to you will never be present in your life again. The sadness feels bottomless, or at least so deep there's nothing there but you and some freaky bioluminescent fish.

Typical thoughts:

"I just can't take this."

"I repeat: I just cannot take this."

5. Acceptance. Maybe you're hoping this is the state of being made whole again, the emotional equivalent of your return being processed and your Visa card being fully credited for the refund—all is as it was before you took a chance on Amazon Essentials bear repellent and lost gruesomely. Look, you're not trying to be an asshole or anything, but you'd just like to go ahead and feel like you used to. Unfortunately, that's probably not in the cards, at least not exactly. You're intact but far from mint condition, a coveted comic book with a few unfortunate scuffs and tears, as well as one bewildering fondue stain. Despite occasional bad days ahead, however, you're ready to reengage with your life, much to the disappointment of your coworker who confiscated your comfy desk chair five minutes after you began bereavement leave.

Typical thoughts:

"I'm grateful for the time that I had with my loved one."

"Look out world, what's left of me is back!"

Of course, not everyone experiences these stages in the same order or experiences them in their entirety at all. And everyone progresses at their own pace, a fact I verified during what I believe is the world's first grief speed run. Since there are only five stages and I'm the definition of a doer, I figured one workday was plenty of time to blast through them. I wrote down everything just as it happened.

GRIEF SPEED RUN

7:00 a.m. Wake up, immediately perform five hundred squat thrusts and five hundred "titan-style" push-ups (one hand planted on ground, one hand crushing marble bust of Zeus to dust).

7:30 a.m. Breakfast of homemade probiotic yogurt while reading seven newspapers (four not in English).

8:15 a.m. Refuse to accept mother's passing. Funny, I am doing this speed run for literally no reason.

8:30 a.m. Shower. Groom hair, beard, and pubic region using proportions Leonardo da Vinci himself recommended in detailed sketches.

10:00 a.m. Dominate first meeting of day like true alpha wolf.

11:55 a.m. Visit men's room prior to next meeting, duck into stall and shriek, "How fucking dare you!" toward the ceiling.

1:00 p.m. Mesmerize clients over oyster lunch.

2:15 p.m. On walk back to office, ponder agonizing possibility that everything might've been different if only I'd picked up on certain things sooner. If only, dammit.

2:30 p.m. Absolutely crush presentation, even by my standards.

3:30 p.m. Remain in darkened conference room afterward and cry. Can this truly be the reality of my life? I just want to shrink down

A Short History of the Never-Released Sixth Stage of Grief

In the decades after Elisabeth Kübler-Ross published her wildly successful five stages model, it seemed as if she was content to simply let her existing contributions to our understanding of grief speak for themselves and withdraw from research. After all, she'd earned tens of millions of dollars from books, paid appearances at nightclub openings and lavish quinceañeras for daughters of Mexican industrialists, and, most profitably, product endorsements. Her 1989 commercial—in which the sixty-three-year-old drives past NBA star Dominique Wilkins for a basket, cracks open an ice-cold Sunkist, and says, "My sixth stage? Refreshment!"—is considered one of the most iconic ads ever. Despite the ad making no actual sense to a single person involved in its production, it did prompt a tantalizing question: would there, could there, ever be a sixth stage of grief? If so, how? Something after acceptance? Shoehorned in between bargaining and depression? The public remained captivated even as Kübler-Ross remained silent.

Then, in early 2004 came the announcement Kübler-Ross fans ("The Küblock," collectively) had been waiting for. The psychologist had engaged with a marketing firm and bought billboards and banner ads with nothing but the number six and the date 8.25.04. It was meant to be cryptic, but everyone knew what the number signified. What else could it be? When word leaked that an outfit called EK-R Enterprises had reserved Madison Square Garden for the very date featured in the six ad campaign, it was all but certain: the sixth stage of grief was on its way, and Elisabeth Kübler-Ross was going big.

A frenzy ensued. People begged their terminally ill loved ones not to die until later in the year, when they could incorporate the new stage into their grieving. Influencers salivated at the prospect of scoring the ultimate inside exclusive—just imagine if Grandma's heart disease pulled the trigger early enough to allow them to be the very first sixth-stage griever. But no one was able to dig up the coveted information, and as it turned out, it didn't matter. Kübler-Ross died on August 24, 2004, one day before her scheduled, epic MSG announcement. She had told no one her sixth stage nor had she written it down. Millions grieved Kübler-Ross's death using her own existing model, which now felt strangely incomplete. And, as ten thousand pounds of unused pyrotechnics were returned to the warehouse and the platform meant for dozens of dancers and several jungle cats was disassembled, an entire world wondered if it could ever truly, fully grieve again.

to nothing and disappear. Anything to make the pain just stop. Just shrink and shrink and shrink.

4:00 p.m. Dash off some emails; pop into boss's office and demand to know his salary since I'll have his job in six months.

5:00 p.m. Leave work, shaken but increasingly convinced that, somehow, I just might get past this.

Again, this accelerated pace may not be for you, but I'm happy to report no ill effects from my grief speed run aside from chronic fatigue, tremors, and a second mouth which has erupted on my back and howls all day and night.

I WISH I HAD DONE TWO OR THREE THINGS BETTER AT MOST: DEALING WITH REGRETS *

We, as a species, have a habit of learning things too late, sometimes tragically so. We surrender thirty years of our lives before realizing we should've been an artist or didn't need to marry the Bath-Salt King of Upper Pensacola. But some of these mistakes, if they can't be undone altogether, are at least reparable after the fact. Who doesn't love one of those heartwarming stories about a senior citizen who was forced to drop out of high school, returns sixty-three years later, and at long

---

* **Sincerity Corner:** There's not a lot I wanted to tell my mother that I didn't actually get around to saying—a long hospital stay, if nothing else, gives you that opportunity. Still, there's part of me that regrets, irrationally, anything I wasn't able to give her in her lifetime. She didn't live to see me get married or make a baby with someone, and if I ever do go through with those things, I'll make sure I botch them so completely that she'd be glad she missed out.

last gives the co-captain of the lacrosse team a hand job?

But death is permanent, which means there's absolutely no fixing things once the Grim Reaper manifests and asks if he can borrow your loved one for a quick sec. Maybe you told them everything you wanted to before they passed, but you probably didn't because there would always be tomorrow and tomorrow's tomorrow for all those weird conversations. Now those unspoken words are just clogging you up, waiting to be repurposed somewhere down the line for your therapist or the poor soul next to you who will never ride a roller coaster alone again. Fortunately, there are ways to at least deal with all you've left on the table.

Remember you're not so bad. Chances are that, for all you never said and wished you had, you didn't leave your loved one with nothing. Maybe you said you loved them, held their hand, or assured them certain documents would be disposed of, as well as the people who know of their existence. When feelings of guilt arise, try to console yourself with what you did accomplish.

Commit to being better. It's too late to send your loved one off with the news that you've stopped gambling or finally discovered that hair gel should not be used internally, but that doesn't mean these changes serve no purpose. Your loved one may not have lived to see these changes, but you can take some comfort in knowing they would have made them happy.

Recognize this was likely inevitable. We try to be diligent, but a few loose ends are just part of this thing we call life. We have every right to expect that our homes will be well-constructed, but we understand that there's always going to be a toilet or two missing. In much the same way, you're saying goodbye to someone you probably had a long and possibly complex relationship with, so there's going to be some stuff that remains unresolved.

VISITING THE GRAVE: TAKING ALL THE FUN OUT OF STARING AT DIRT

In the movies, the weather at the grave is either perfect or a drenching downpour, and maybe a visiting protagonist lays a tidy bouquet on the headstone in such a way that it doesn't cover a single letter of the inscription. Then they articulate their feelings out loud, even if they're alone, so we've got some insight into their motivation, something like, "I let you down, Mama" or "I'm sorry I thought it'd be fun to take a pedicab to the emergency room." But in real life, these visits can be uncertain, awkward. What are they actually supposed to be like?

Fortunately, others have gone before you, and I mean that literally. Not only that, but, like a hotel or seafood "shack" that sells forty dollar lobster rolls, they've also posted reviews of the experience on various travel sites. So, before you visit your loved one's grave, maybe see what others who also visited had to say first. For example, here are some online reviews from the grave of Michelle Naylor, a St. Louis-area woman who died reasonably loved in 2015.

Decent enough
* * *
Pretty standard. Fine for my aunt, who was just sort of average. I think it might be good enough for my uncle to be buried next to one day, but I'd probably check out some other spots first if I were him.

Rating Grief with the Chili Pepper System

The chili pepper icon is a familiar sight on the menus of casual dining Mexican restaurants everywhere, signifying that, watch out, there may be some flavor in the accompanying entrée. The pepper rating so intuitively conveys vital information about what to expect from enchiladas that no one would ever suspect that it was actually first employed by grief counselors. But for decades, in fact, these professionals have used the peppers as a diagnostic shorthand that helps them tailor treatment to how much a client's grief brings the heat.

- 🌶 : Just a zing of unhappiness that adds complexity to someone's ordinary emotional state without totally overwhelming it.

- 🌶🌶: Now this grief packs a punch! You'll get through it OK, but you'd better pace yourself.

- 🌶🌶🌶: *Picante* and then some, this is scorching grief that will test even those who've lost loved ones before and overconfidently think they can handle it.

- 🌶🌶🌶🌶: Reserved for grief so potent, it can leave someone crying uncontrollably or even unable to speak. There's a reason it's called El Corazón Muerto and that people experiencing it sometimes have to sign a waiver before they can even talk about it in therapy.

Had a BLAST!
*****

I got there thinking it'd be kind of solemn, but mind blown. My only regret is that my grandma didn't die in her sleep sooner!

Just OK
**

You get to the grave, and there's no greeter or host or anything like that so you're pretty much on your own. There also wasn't anywhere to sit. I love my sister, but I probably won't be back for a while.

Fine for passing 20 minutes or so
***

My aunt's headstone is lovely, but the grounds are a little scraggly and you can hear what sounds like an auto body shop like a hundred feet away. Not sure I'd go if I wasn't already in the area picking up some cabinet hinges at Home Depot.

Almost perfecto!
****

Really beautifully situated with a totally classy headstone and just the right amount of shade. The only reason I'm not giving it five stars is that it's on a hill, and I'm pretty sure a bad rain is going to wash my mother into the Gulf of Mexico.

So frickin' boooooooring
*

Honestly, I was just counting the minutes until I left. Maybe I would've liked it more if I knew who this person was, not sure.*

---

* **Sincerity Corner:** I haven't visited my mother's grave since the day she was low-ered into it. Partly because it's on the other side of the country and partly because the pandemic made getting out there impossible. But honestly, I don't know if that would be the best way for me to connect with her regardless. I have old voicemails she's left me, and I feel like I'm better off checking in with her that way, when she was alive and wishing me a happy new year or telling me what restaurants from my childhood had closed down. Of course, I could just be a little afraid.

DEAD MAN'S JEANS:
DEALING WITH BELONGINGS

We all remember that gut-wrenching moment in *The Lion King* when Mufasa dies, and how Simba spends the final forty-five minutes of the movie trying to figure out what to do with his father's old sneakers. That's because when we die, we simply abandon a lot of stuff—stuff we actively used, accumulated stuff we just never got around to throwing out, stuff we hoped to weigh our children down with someday. But when your loved one passed, even if they took pains in a will to make sure their most valuable property went to their least worthless next of kin, odds are they left behind plenty, and totally unsorted. Where is it all going to go?

Everyday items like your mother's perfume 'for the wicked retiree' can be surprisingly triggering.

And that's not even the most difficult part. Everything would be simpler if you were just dealing with a pile-up of trash. Then it'd be as easy as luring a hoarder out of his apartment for five minutes while you dispose of three hundred pounds of pizza boxes and set free the feral cat colony. But when someone dies, they often leave behind a life in progress: glasses on the nightstand, a jacket on the usual hook, a romance novel bookmarked halfway through (which fortunately means your loved one at least got to read the part where Vivienne Lark gets absolutely reamed by a sexy buccaneer). Your loved one died, but their belongings are still ready to pick up where they left off. Their favorite chair almost seems to be waiting for the familiar buttocks which gave it purpose. And that puts you in the sad and bizarre position of, in a sense, breaking the news to these objects, of capping the toothpaste tube that's expecting the usual squeeze around 10:30. Which, of course, is another way of microdosing the bad news yourself all over again. So, aside from your loved one coming back for their stuff with some celestial storage pod, how can you deal with all the possessions that aren't going to move an inch on their own?

If you're unlucky, you'll have to move fast. Maybe your loved one's house is being sold, or their landlord needs the apartment cleaned out in a hurry so he can get rolling on overcharging a new tenant. But if you've got some time, then feel free to leave things where they are until you're ready to make some decisions. Because they may not be easy decisions. You'll have to think things through, much more than you did when you went to a college based entirely on an ad you saw shaved into the side of a dog. And when the time comes, you'll have five groups to put things in.

Keep. This group includes belongings you'd like to hold onto and belongings you convince yourself you'd like to hold onto but which you'll drag out to the curb in about a month's time. This group may also include possessions you do not want but that your loved one wanted you to want and that you'll throw in your car out of sheer abiding love. You'll figure out what exactly to do with the western hemisphere's largest collection of Virgin Mary-themed TV trays some other day.

Sell. Sounds crass, doesn't it? And I guess it can be if you're just hawking your mother's engagement ring at the closest pawn shop and heading straight to the cosmetic surgeon for a procedure called scrotal resurrection. But once you've set aside items of sentimental value, you'll still be left with others that you aren't as connected with emotionally and that your loved one would probably *want* you to sell— that car whose oil they didn't get changed until it curdled into acidic sludge and ate through the dashboard? Go ahead and get anything you can for it with a clear conscience. Remember, what's so fantastic about grief is that you're certain to find something else to feel guilty about down the line.

Donate. Here's where you'll put items you unfortunately don't have room for (i.e. absolutely do not want) but that can be of use to people in need. It's a comfort to know you can offload onto a thrift store the "vase" your loved one made in pottery class that just looks like clay screaming. If it helps, you can imagine your loved one's pill organizer and baggie of assorted rusty fishhooks giving a struggling family the Christmas they didn't think they'd have this year.

Trash. Sad to say you can't burden charity with everything, which means you're going to have to put real belongings from your loved one into real trash bags. Of course, some of it was headed there soon enough anyway—that half of a roast beef sandwich your loved one left in the fridge was never going to be passed down and worn by their granddaughter on her wedding day. Still, throwing things away can feel like you're conceding something to death you're not ready to concede, even if death instantly moved on from your loved one to a tourist at Yellowstone who antagonized one elk too many. That's why it can be tremendously useful to have a friend or more distant family member lend a hand. Assuming they're careful enough to not tread upon too many heirlooms and tactful enough to refrain from observing, "It's like I'm exploring a pharaoh's tomb, if pharaohs only made fifty grand a year," you can lean on them to help out with the more emotionally charged tasks you might not be up for.

Give the Grass Lord His Due. The Grass Lord, you may discover, is a minor magical creature that your loved one signed a pact with in order to attain some equally insignificant goal—a convenient parking space, a Wingstop-branded hoodie, thirty seconds with a proportionate forehead. Upon your loved one's death, the creature will expect to have his tribute laid out for him on a nearby grassy area, such as the backyard or a neighborhood park. The payment is typically one piece of silver, although it is often ignored in practice. When it comes down to it, the Grass Lord is terrified of confrontation.

I WOULDN'T GRIEVE IF HE DIED TWICE: GRIEF AND TOXIC RELATIONSHIPS

What if on their deathbed, your "loved one" took your hand and said, "I wish it were you dying today but, fingers crossed, today isn't over yet"? Maybe you'd attribute it to pain or delirium until you recalled they've told you the very same thing over and over, made a point to tell you every year on your birthday, and waited until your friends showed up for your party to do it. So, yeah, you're thinking about sitting grief out this time around, though others are welcome to it if they insist. Like you're obligingly kicking back at home when your friends go out to a movie you've already seen.

And yet, there's this nagging feeling, this persistent, irritating tingle in the back of your brain telling you that you really ought to cough up at least a little grief: a frown, a catch in the throat, a moment of distraction that you snap out of with, "Sorry, I'm just having trouble concentrating these days because I am ever so shattered." It's the thing to do, and maybe other people in your life are doing it, after all. Granted, the deceased didn't make a habit of telling them that they should drop everything and get a face transplant, but you still feel the pull of the expectation. You feel it despite the fact that your anger was never dissolved in any way. The closest you ever got to an apology was, "I'm sorry. By which I mean I'm sorry your existence disproved God's." So maybe, *maybe*, you can stand stone-faced for the duration of a funeral, but how long should you be expected to keep up appearances? Should you be expected to do such a thing in the first place?

If someone was truly toxic—not good mixed with bad, but bad mixed with hideous—chances are you're not the only one who suffered. In that case, there might be little confusion or outrage about why your eulogy was simply, "Peace out, dirtbag!" and why you're jamming the casket with a broomstick handle so it gets lowered into Hell that much faster. But if you were singled out in the worst ways, you might feel alone in your resentment and even not deserving of it. It helps to recall at these moments that, as therapists often say, grief is as particular as a customized Cameo video from *The Office*'s Brian Baumgartner, which is just a fancy psychobabble way of saying that other people's feelings don't dictate yours. Maybe, over time—lots of time, so much time your hair is gray and you've got two teeth wondering where the other thirty went—you can find your way to forgiveness and take a connecting train to grief. That can be cleansing, restorative. Or maybe you won't, now or ever. Remember that just because someone's dead doesn't mean you owe them the payoff. But, hey, maybe you'll get around to grieving in the next life.

Requiem for an Iguana: Grieving for Pets

This book is intended primarily for humans mourning other humans. Just because, you know, that's the standard arrangement. But people will form emotional attachments to almost anything if you give them the chance—football teams, their country, a limited-time fast-food beef variation—and grieve when those things are taken from them. So of course we grieve when we lose the dogs who loved us and the cats who bore us no obvious ill will. The loss can cut deep even with smaller, stupider creatures. Sure, your goldfish gagged to death on its own waste because you didn't clean its bowl for a month, but you still feel that hurt. Essentially, our pets are—in their furry, feathered, or mucus-secreting way—our loved ones too. One of the most poignant testaments to this bond is the famous "Rainbow Bridge" prose poem, which I've decided to simply reproduce in its entirety here.

Just this side of Heaven is a place called Rainbow Bridge.

When an animal dies that has been especially close to someone here, that pet goes to Rainbow Bridge. There is plenty of food, water, and sunshine, and our friends are warm and comfortable. If their genitals were removed in life, they have been restored in triplicate.

All the animals who had been ill and old are restored to health and vigor. Those who were hurt or maimed are made whole and strong again through cybernetic enhancements—still the pet you loved, yes, but so much more, now capable of up to a thousand billion calculations per second. The animal perfected.

The animals are happy and content, except for one small thing; they each miss someone very special to them, a human by the name of [**Most versions of the poem have a list of a hundred first names that readers can choose from here. If a reader's name is unlisted, they should assume their pet is now thoroughly at peace with their absence.**].

The animals all run and play together, but the day comes when one suddenly stops and looks into the distance. Suddenly he begins to run from the group, his legs carrying him faster and faster. Assume, of course, that birds are flying and that slower pets like turtles are being transported as a courtesy on the backs of faster animals.

You have been spotted and forgiven for not having taken your own life years ago in solidarity. You cling together in joyous reunion, never to be parted again.

Then you cross Rainbow Bridge together. In Heaven, however, all pets require an additional six hundred dollar deposit, and any dogs over twenty-five pounds are strictly prohibited.
                                                                                    —Author Unknown

Grief Journal Prompts

1. Were you satisfied with the funeral you planned? If not, was it a terrible mistake to trust you?

2. Visualize your grief as a painting. Would it sell for more than Damien Hirst's seventeen million dollar tiger shark preserved in formaldehyde?

3. Think of something that you're grateful you told your loved one before they died. Or, if there's something you wish you'd told them but didn't, write it down and see if a bird or flying insect will deliver it to the afterlife.

4. What bit of good news might you share with your loved one at their grave? If you don't have any good news, which of the following fabrications would you feel most comfortable sharing?
   "I got a promotion at work."
   "We're pregnant."
   "I got assigned a judge with a lenient reputation."
   "It is not syphilis at all, but something entirely alien in origin."

n early 2022, this sterile worker ant suffered an almost incomprehensible tragedy. More than one hundred thousand of its sisters were killed when a riding lawn mower ground its colony nearly to dust. It wondered, like you, perhaps, how it could go on foraging for fungus and milking aphids for their sugar-rich secretions. But rather than succumb to its pain, this ant chose to heal itself by helping others do so. The result is *Strong as an Ant*.

In this heartfelt work, available exclusively as a pheromone smear, the ant reflects on the struggles it faced and the lessons it learned as it confronted its new and frightening world. Although originally written for ants, the hard-earned wisdom in this collection has also transformed the way quadrillions of bees, wasps, and other invertebrates approach their own grief. And now you can discover hope, inspiration, and even a touch of laughter from a six-week-old black ant who lost so much but refused to lose itself.

Here are just some of the things this extraordinary work can help you with:

- Moving ahead day by day when you don't think you'll ever have the mandible strength to tunnel through a rotting log again.
- Accepting that life, even if you're lucky enough to live twelve months, will never be exactly the same again.
- Finding comfort in small pleasures, like swarming over a baby lizard.
- Taking the time to appreciate the preciousness of life even when you're back to "normal" and enslaving the offspring from neighboring ant colonies.

You may think you just can't bear your grief anymore, but there's at least one insect who knows otherwise. Whether you know it or not, you're not just strong—you're *Strong as an Ant*.

PUPA PRESS
"Books by Insects for the World"

CHAPTER III

OTHER PEOPLE: THE HELPFUL, THE RIDICULOUS, THE USELESS

People. What are they, and where do they come from? No one knows. But a fair number of them are probably going to be making an appearance as you grieve. Like the layer of soggy leaves you suddenly find blanketing your car after a thunderstorm, you'll eventually have to decide which people to sweep onto the street with your wipers and which ones you're OK with leaving stuck to the hood for the time being. And that's not as easy as it seems. People reveal themselves in moments like these.* The coworker you thought was good for nothing more than stealing your ideas and grotesquely ripping apart a rotisserie chicken at his desk might surprise you with stunning kindness. Meanwhile, the person you thought was your best friend might be the one who shows up fifty minutes late to the funeral still soaked in sweat from a fitness class called Turbo Glute.

Some people will find out about the passing of your loved one from word of mouth, the social media post you'll learn to craft later in this chapter, or the jet-black candy that pours out the belly of your death-reveal piñata. Others, unfortunately, are going to have to find out from you directly. How can you manage that awkward moment? And how can you navigate interpersonal settings without falling to your knees and sobbing into someone's crotch, especially if you did that several times daily *before* your loved one died?

---

* **Sincerity Corner:** I find it fascinating how this moment smudges the boundaries of certain relationships. How our relationships with, say, a coworker or drinking buddy or friendly next-door neighbor are briefly forced to acknowledge our deeper human torments before, oddly enough, snapping right back into place.

THE OVERCROWDED SUBWAY PLATFORM
OF LOVE: YOUR SUPPORT SYSTEM

Some things can easily be accomplished all by yourself—brushing your teeth, signing your name, or falling into a leopard habitat while taking a selfie at the zoo. But you might find that grieving with the help of a support system—people who can ease your pain when you're low on sedative money—is the way to go. Who are these people, and what can you realistically expect from them?

Family. We all know the hostility that arises when we hold up the line at the rental car counter for two hours because they were unable to fulfill our request for the exact vehicle Jerry Seinfeld and Bill Maher drove in an episode of *Comedians in Cars Getting Coffee*. That's because, whatever their previous differences, the people waiting behind us have now united in pure, single-minded hatred. Grief's like that in a way. Whatever our differences with our family, there's really no one else who truly grasps how we're feeling at this very moment. It will be a crucial bond at this time, but bear in mind that your family members' own grief might limit the amount of help they can offer. Allow them the space to do what they're capable of, and if you've always had low expectations for them to begin with, so much the better. You also might find that helping them heal also helps *you* heal in much the same way that helping a child find her lost puppy entitles you to owning it part-time.

Friends. It really is like that song from the show—"*I'll be there for you, when the rain starts to fall because your beloved grandmother finally passes after being unable to recover from a cluster of strokes.*" Of course, if they're at all acquainted with your loved one, your friends might be in some

A Letter to Your Friend Who Wants to Help but Doesn't Know How

Your friends want to be there for you at this awful moment. But they're wary. It's possible they haven't yet experienced grief themselves and don't know what exactly to say or do. They can just imagine the shock and disgust on your face as you behold their well-intentioned RIP cold-cut arrangement. You might try to help them by verbally articulating your feelings using common grief metaphors ("It's like a howler monkey pulling your heart out of your chest and going to town on it like a mango" or "Imagine the worst day of your life and now multiply that by Satan"). But you also have the option of sparing them and yourself an awkward conversation by simply writing them a heartfelt letter that reassures them and lets them know exactly what you hope they'll do for you. Once you take the uncomfortable ambiguity out of the equation, you'll find your friends are ready and eager to lend a hand.

Dear Valued Friend:

I've sent you this letter as a courtesy on the occasion of my loved one's passing. You might be wondering how to interact with me at this difficult moment, especially since I may not know entirely myself—after all, how does one truly prepare for their loved one's [CIRCLE ONE] heart attack/mortal wounds sustained from overestimating martial arts prowess/utter tumor fiasco. I hope this note will put you at ease. The last thing I want is for my tough time to extend to the people I care about.

Honestly, all I need from you right now is to fasten the titanium bracelet which accompanied this letter around your wrist, bearing in mind that once it's in place, an explosion will be required to remove it. The advanced GPS chip within the bracelet will allow me to track your movements twenty-four hours a day, even in tunnels or the remote wilderness. The embedded speakers will allow me to communicate with you verbally or to simply trigger an alarm of five hundred decibels (about four ambulance sirens), and the proprietary pain tech will help ensure you obey my commands. You might want to move within five miles of my home to ensure prompt compliance if I require your physical presence. I may never or may constantly. What is certain is that testing me would be a mistake.

Anyway, I guess we're both figuring this out together. But we will! I hope you'll bear with me. And whatever happens, thank you, thank you, thank you for being my friend!

pain themselves, but they're going to have to process that on their own time because they need to step up and soak up your sadness like a quality bath rug. Whether it's being a shoulder to cry on, taking you to a movie, or cooking you a hot meal when you just don't have the energy to slaughter a goat, your friends will be an invaluable resource. And you shouldn't be bashful about leaning on them either. When the time comes, they'll turn to you, and you'll wish you'd gotten thousands in uncompensated labor from them when you had the chance.

Strangers. You might think of a stranger as a passer-by on the street, another commuter on the bus, or the person who's greeted you in the mirror since you turned thirty and lost track of everything that was supposed to matter. But strangers can be an unexpected source of comfort. Sometimes it can help to just sit quietly in a coffee shop among people oblivious to your pain as they work or read or come to terms with how their date's profile pic told a dozen separate lies. And you never know when you'll find yourself sharing an unexpected connection with a stranger who might have lost someone as well. You can't manufacture these moments, of course, but you can give serendipity a little boost by slipping gentle prompts into everyday conversation.

"Excuse me, did the 37 bus come by yet? Also, I can't believe it's already been four months since the funeral."

"I'll go ahead and try the bisque. Also, isn't it weird how long it takes for the permanence of death to truly sink in?"

"You think you're doing OK, but then the sadness hits you all of a sudden, and you don't even know what prompted it. Then you realize that just may be how things are from now on. And maybe that's fine. Because it's a reminder

of how lucky you were to have had this person in your life and to have loved someone so deeply. Anyway, one ticket for Space Jam 2, *please."*

Grief Counselors. If I recall the novel's characters correctly, it's fair to describe your grief as your Moby Dick and this invaluable book as your Ahab, who tracks down, kills, and eats the white whale in the first chapter. But you may choose to supplement this resource with the help of a professional, someone who not only has experience working with people in precisely your state of emotional disrepair but also the clinical detachment that's absolutely essential for charging you two hundred dollars an hour. But how do you find the right grief counselor? Unfortunately, you can't just wait for a therapist aroused by the irresistible musk of your anguish to track you down. You need a plan.

Step 1: Check with your insurance provider to find out which minuscule fraction of available practitioners accept your policy. You'll likely eliminate 80 percent right off the top and can then focus on the inexperienced or desperate ones who remain. (Some therapists do offer a sliding scale that might reduce an outrageous charge to something much more manageably out of reach.)

Step 2: Just as not every teacher teaches the alphabet in the exact same order, not every therapist does their work in the same way. They might gently guide you toward insights in a traditional talk therapy setting, focus on helping you make concrete adjustments to your thoughts and actions in the here and now, or softly tap a miniature gong while you caress a mannequin that's wearing your own clothes. So it's important, even before you get to their couch, that you find out what their approach to treatment is. If it's not quite right for you, keep looking. By the time you're on your sixth year of something called "cathartic shriek yo-yo," you might be too invested or exhausted to seek out someone else.

Step 3: Inquire about the therapist's professional experience with grief. Is it a specialty or at least a significant part of their practice, or will you have to be the one to sit them down and delicately explain that everyone—yes, even their puppy—will one day die?

Step 4: Consider other factors. Do you want your therapist to be male or female? Or what about their age? Would you prefer someone older who might fall asleep at your most vulnerable moment or a younger therapist who might be livestreaming your session on social media with nothing more than the caption, "Today's episode of Despondent Loser Crybaby 😭 😭 😭" Or maybe one-on-one therapy isn't right for you at all, and you'd benefit more from a group therapy setting, which can provide you with camaraderie as well as an opportunity to aggressively, almost threateningly, promote this book to others.

THE BEREAVEMENT BOWL: COMPETITIVE GRIEF

We've seen the inspirational footage before. A marathon runner is exhausted. He's made it twenty-six grueling miles, but his shaky legs will simply not allow him to complete that last 0.2. He's done. This is as far as—but wait! Another runner who'd been running briskly nearby stops in his tracks. He makes his way over and throws the other man's arm over his shoulder. Then the two of them, together, shuffle as one to the finish line. It's touching because it exemplifies our human capacity for selflessness and the true spirit of athletics. But an overlooked aspect of this scenario is that the two men in question are actually sweaty losers. That's because in America—and this is still America last time I confirmed my address

What Do I Do With Sympathy Cards?

Sympathy just hasn't kept up with our evolving technology. Sure, it's not out of the question these days to receive a string of alternating heart and tombstone emojis, but for the most part, condolences still haven't gone paperless. And when the cards start coming in, what do you do then? That all depends on the card.

Premium Card with Thought-Out, Heartfelt Message
This person obviously didn't buy their card at the same CVS where they purchased Mucinex, and they took the time to write specifically about how your loved one made an impact on their life. Maybe keep this around and turn to it when you inevitably need a few words of warmth.

Generic Card with Generic Condolence
Playing it safe with the floral-pattern Hallmark and innocuous "With deepest sympathy" message. No harm done. Custom demanded that they send you a card, and they followed through before a distasteful amount of time had passed. Keep, throw out, it's all the same.

Generic Card Whose Condolences Trail Off into a Message to Someone Else
The person writing this card couldn't be bothered to give your loss even a minute of undivided attention before digressing into an unrelated personal or professional matter. "Your father was always so generous to my whole family and needs to get on the same page as Connie at the warehouse ASAP because this inventory situation is about to make my sales guys shit themselves." Straight in trash.

Card with Shrek Saying, "I'm Watchin' Your Husband in Purgatory!"
Shocking to say the least, even without the bizarre implication that the character Shrek is real, is dead, has still not yet qualified for Heaven, and is actively monitoring your husband, who has apparently not qualified for Heaven either. Doesn't really matter what you do with this card since the person who sent it is also the type of person who will send you a duplicate every day for the rest of your life.

A Short History of Grief Counselors

Today, finding a qualified grief counselor is as easy as going online or putting up a flyer with your phone number and a picture of your tear-streaked face. But people suffered from grief long before there were therapists to help them cope with it. Instead of talking about their feelings with trained professionals, our prehistoric ancestors might have retreated into the wilderness and howled into a hollow log, muffled their sobs on the flanks of a giant sloth, or just repressed their emotions until an elder with a sharpened rock could be summoned to scoop out the part of the heart where the sad feelings were hiding.

But with the dawn of agriculture came an end to nomadic life and a newfound need for as much labor as possible to tend the fields. This meant fewer opportunities to wander into the ocean in order to cry for one's favorite aunt on an isolated offshore sandbar. With people living more localized, sedentary lives, grief became more visible. A new specialized trade arose, comprised of individuals who were too emo for fieldwork but who had a knack for listening and being empathetic. While these so-called "comfort herdsmen" had relatively low social status and were eaten first in times of famine, they nevertheless represented the emergence of grief expertise.

But as time went on, the prestige of the grief counselor grew. They stood at the sides of kings, who would turn to them for consolation after sending ten thousand soldiers armed with sticks to die at the hands of ten thousand soldiers armed with five hundred thousand additional soldiers. Grief counselors became the means by which the kings unburdened themselves and found the strength to launch all-new bloody conflicts. As a result, grief counselors became some of the most despised people in all of civilization. To even utter the words, "It's OK to be hurting," ran the risk of being torn apart by a mob.

Grief counselors did not reenter the mainstream until the mid-twentieth century, when Geneviève, the beloved endangered rhino born in captivity at the Paris zoo died suddenly from complications during an ill-advised lap-band surgery. An entire nation was simply unable to process this loss on its own, which was weird considering they'd handled two world wars pretty OK. In any case, emergency authorizations lifted the sanctions on grief counselors that had existed for centuries, and allowed them to resume their healing craft. If you have worked with a grief therapist recently, now you know why they gently kiss a small rhino figurine before each session.

to PayPal—winning is everything. And, unfortunately, that can even be true with grief.

Most people, even spectacular dum-dums, will do their best to be supportive when you talk about your grief. They may not entirely succeed, of course. They might say you're fortunate that your loved one didn't die years ago with that kind of berserk obesity or that you should take comfort in the knowledge they'll be reincarnated as one of the heartier insects. But then there are others who regard grief as a zero-sum game, not something we all just miserably take turns at. Their goal, at least on the surface, seems to be putting up more points on the grief scoreboard. Consider the replies in the following exchanges:

EXCHANGE 1

"I can't believe my uncle's gone. I'll miss him so much."

"Poor you. Get back to me when your mother dies from Alzheimer's a full three years after forgetting she's potty-trained."

EXCHANGE 2

"I just can't believe that I'm not going to get a call from my dad on Christmas this year. I'm absolutely dreading the holiday I used to love."

"Big deal. I lost the Mace Windu bishop from my Attack of the Clones commemorative chess set, and I can't even find a replacement on eBay for less than a hundred bucks."

While not coming right out and saying, "I find your sadness a nuisance," these replies do share a lack of consideration for where the griever is at, turning the moment back on themselves. But in the first case at least, the respondent might be speaking from a place of immersion in their own grief. The second reply—one most grievers eventually confront, though not all with the same Jedi—is just a callously shortsighted attempt at one-upmanship. Fundamentally, replies like these are misguided efforts at giving you perspective instead of comfort, which may cause you to second-guess your own grief with thoughts like:

- *"Maybe I should just get over it already."*
- *"Wow, she has it way worse than I do. It's actually pretty rad that my grandpa's gone."*
- *"He's right. I shouldn't be sad. I should feel lucky that my father died surrounded by his family at home and not from slipping on a Bichon Frise and breaking his neck while streaking the Westminster Dog Show."*

Ultimately, you are entitled to your feelings, even if they don't slot in perfectly with the hierarchy in someone's else emotional org chart. When you think about all the opportunities you have to fail, all the many ways you can come up short and humiliatingly so, you realize that your grief doesn't have to be one of them.

EXTRA! EXTRA! GRANDPA PASSED AWAY QUIETLY LAST NIGHT! SHARING THE BAD NEWS

Describing something that happened to you is a way of reliving it, and that's great if you're recounting good news like finding ten bucks on the sidewalk or finally turning your back on ISIS. But the death of a loved one is different. Each time you tell someone, you briefly revisit that painful moment. Many people describe this feeling as like letting a heavyset squirrel sit on an existing bruise. So how can you break the news in such a way that spares you and others as much discomfort as possible?

Social Media

Before we had social media to slip a death announcement into someone's online ticker of cat pics and menacing Second Amendment memes, it wasn't easy to announce a loved one's passing. But we didn't really need to. Our worlds have been much smaller for most of our history. If someone died, there was a pretty good chance everyone they knew watched it happen and then just decided as a group which cemetery, quicksand pit, or scavenger animals would claim the body. Now, of course, our connections are far-flung. However, thanks to social media, particularly Facebook, we can tell hundreds of people at once that someone they loved, liked, or never got around to unfollowing has sadly passed on. And that's why it's essential to get it right.

Believe it or not, announcing a death on social media takes more preparation than typing, "The cutest!!" beneath a photo of your nephew's, let's be honest, lazy Halloween costume. Before you put that cursor anywhere near the text field, keep in mind that close relatives and friends should never be notified via Facebook. Anyone who stands to be shattered by the news should have zero chance of receiving it on the same platform they just took a "Which Spider-Man Villain Are You?" quiz.

After making sure that the people who should know in advance do know in advance, you're ready to write your post. While your most difficult Facebook moment used to be that time you accidentally entered your Google search for "is hamburger found in ocean edible" in your status bar, I'm afraid that's about to change.

The Text

Composing these sentences will feel strange. Your reluctance will be palpable. Your hands might feel heavy, like there's a lasagna strapped to each of them. So take your time.* Close your laptop and go for a walk. Jump on another app. If you're on a library terminal, feel free to use every minute of the half hour you signed up for, no matter how impatient the man behind you is to test the limits of the computer's pornography filter.

You can never fully prepare readers for this sort of news, but you should at least set the stage immediately with a solemn opening, such as, "It is with great sadness that I announce the passing of..." or "It's with the heaviest of hearts that our family announces the passing of..." Heartfelt simplicity is best, but people too often get caught up in unneeded complexity:

"According to data from the National Cancer Institute (NCI), pancreatic cancer was projected to claim the lives of approximately 45,750 Americans in 2022, with only lung cancer and colorectal cancer killing more. Last night, my uncle became one of them."

---

* **Sincerity Corner:** After years of using my Facebook feed for posting pictures of my cat's unstoppable weight gain and recycling jokes that had humiliatingly underperformed on Twitter, it was weird to suddenly be in the position of actually thinking through a post. Here's what I posted, along with a picture of my mom as a young woman graduating nursing school: "We said goodbye to my mother, Phyllis, over the weekend. If I've ever done anything kind for you, she's the reason why. If I haven't, I'll try harder to remember what she taught me. This is her on the verge of a lifetime of helping and healing others." Ironically, she would've been the one person to click Like no matter how much it underwhelmed and would've commented, "I love it!" even if I'd cropped half her face out.

Off-putting casualness:
"It's official! The Denver Broncos are choke artists!!! I'm glad Dad wasn't around to see this pathetic loss because, as it happens, he died last night."

Or totally unnecessary and anxiety-producing ambiguity:
"Come to Traylor Funeral Home on Saturday at 10 a.m. and discover for yourself which of my aunts passed away this morning!"

Now comes the trickier part: figuring out what you want to say about your loved one. Before you start stringing sentences together, maybe grab a pen and paper and just jot down whatever words come to mind.

- Loving wife, mother, and grandmother.

- Dedicated teacher for more than thirty years.

- Cruel sometimes, mostly when she drank, but not exclusively. The source of my body dysmorphia for sure. I'm glad she conquered her demons later in life, but, while I'll grieve her loss now, I also grieve for the mother I wish she had been much sooner.

- Number-one dog lover.

While all these items may be true, the third one may be too revealing for an audience of more peripheral friends and relatives, and upsetting to more intimate relations. Instead, air these more complicated thoughts in a therapy setting or use them as fuel for lashing out at a waitress for seemingly no reason whatsoever.

The Photo

Look at the two photos below. Which do you think would be more appropriate for a memorial post?

The answer? It depends, actually, because you want a photo that truly embodies who your loved one was. Maybe she was a conventional dresser, or maybe she wore raunchy tees for seventy-five years in tribute to the kindly Russian soldier who liberated her from the Nazis and kept her warm by wrapping her in a "Horny All Day, Porkin' All Night" tank top. In other words, worry less about what's expected and more about what would make your loved one feel authentically seen and appreciated. And don't hesitate to post more than one photo. For example, pairing a photo from an elder's youth with a more current one is a beautiful way to bookend their life and remind younger people how all their vitality is going to work out for them in the end.

Face to Face

But there are limits to the blast radius of social media. For example, we all know people too precious to let Mark Zuckerberg gorge himself on their personal data or who just don't see the appeal of staying in touch with film club weirdos they abandoned after two meetings a decade ago. And even if people *have* found out, there's still that moment when the death has to be acknowledged in conversation regardless. It's a gruesomely uncomfortable exchange in which both you and the person you're speaking with are quietly praying for anything—a phone call, a sinkhole directly beneath your feet—that might interrupt it. How can you best manage these situations?

If You Need Me, I'll Be Wailing in the Supply Closet: Grief at Work
You can safely assume that by the time you return from bereavement leave, at least some of your coworkers will have gotten the news. (That is, if you're fortunate enough to have bereavement leave and not just a boss warning you not to take your personal problems out on customers who don't want your tears in their burrito bowl.) You won't know who's up to date on your situation because you won't know exactly how that information was circulated. An announcement in a small departmental meeting? An all-staff email blast? A single lily mysteriously laid across your workstation? This means it's possible that at least a few people will assume nothing's amiss. And you're certainly not obligated to disclose the truth.

COWORKER: *"Hey, buddy. Haven't seen you around in a while."*

YOU: *"Yeah, I was doing some traveling, but never once attended a funeral."*

Soon however, you'll encounter the coworkers who *do* know. You'll feel the tension immediately. Some might avoid eye contact or just pretend you're not there even more than usual. It's not that they're unkind. They're just not sure what you want from them at this moment. Maybe you'd be boosted in some small way by a few expressions of condolence or just want to plunge right back into the day-to-day or would really feel comforted by a couple of your enemies being let go without severance. And while some of your colleagues will take the initiative, many will wait to take their cue from you. Just talk about work, and they will too. Post a sign-up sheet outside your office for hugs or something ominously called "sympathy tickles," and it'll likely be filled out in no time.

Incidentally, while work might be a welcome distraction from the abyss, being surrounded by so many people can also be difficult. You never know who or what is going to trigger you. Maybe someone in accounting has a laugh that reminds you of your mother, or your boss is wearing three of your father's neckties. Whatever it is, have a plan. If you suddenly need to cry, is there some private location—a restroom, a stairwell, even a bucket you can gently lower over your head—where you can discreetly spend a few minutes? Or maybe there's a colleague you're close with who can take a little time away from the work necessary to feed their family and just sit with you. If so, don't hesitate to ask.

So, What Do You Like to Do When You're Not Inconsolable?
Grief on a Date
On one hand, dating might be the very last thing on your mind right now. It's hard to take happy hour seriously when you can still hear the sound of dirt being dumped upon your loved one's casket lid. Still, maybe it would be helpful to distract yourself with some company, and you can just add your grief to the list of things you were ultimately planning on burdening any future partner with anyway. But how do you navigate a date when, lurking behind your only good shirt, is a terrible sense of loss?

Common Condolences, Ranked

Even if people offer a nonverbal form of support, maybe a quick hug or a lengthy tongue bath, there's no way around a spoken expression of sympathy. As they reach out to you in the weeks after the death of your loved one, you'll want to put their condolences into ranked tiers so you'll know exactly how much to resent them going forward.

Tier 1: Solid Compassion
"I'm so sorry for your loss."
"I'm not sure what to say, but I care."

Tier 2: Well-Intentioned Dipshit Talk
"This was God's plan."
"Time heals all wounds."

Tier 3: Making It So Much Worse
"If you need me, it'd really streamline things if you went through my assistant."
"Don't worry, you'll be reunited in nothingness someday."
"As someone who recently dropped his phone in the toilet, I know how you feel."
"If it's any consolation, I'm feeling super-duper."

Tier 4: Basic Human Decency Is Beyond Them
"This was God's plan. He told me months ago, and I deliberately didn't tell you."
"Tonight I'm popping the champagne I bought just for this occasion. I don't mean just one bottle."
"Remember, the only pain your grandmother's feeling now is what the devil is inflicting."
"I'm actively rumormongering in hopes that your uncle will have to be reburied in a cemetery that accepts notorious sex offenders."

Marcie 29
📍 12 miles away

About Me: I recently cremated an immediate family member.

"While it's perfectly acceptable to reveal your grief later, along with your crushing debt and lifetime ban from the LEGO Store, you should also feel free to disclose it right away."

Put It Out There Early. If you're on the apps, you can simply let people know up front that you're game but struggling a bit. Sure, some of them will be driven off, but there might be others who've been in your shoes or who find your pain the sweetest aphrodisiac.

Nervously Tap-Dance around the Topic. Dates, especially early on, are brimming with distortions. When you're out of work, you're "freelancing." When you've tested positive for STDs, you've tested "negative" for STDs, and so on. So unless you're asked a point-blank question—like, "Who in your immediate family is alive as of right this minute?"—you don't have to volunteer anything. And if the very subject of family is a raw nerve at the moment, you can just deflect. For example, if your date asks if your parents still live in Houston, you have every right to nudge the conversation toward safer ground by responding with, "I'd be more interested in hearing a twenty-seventh time about your metabolism supplement startup" or "My views about 9/11 are considered controversial even within the larger truther community."

Put It Out There Late. In the end, you might realize you're not ready for dating only when you're sulking in front of your barely touched margarita and wishing the jukebox was playing the voice of your loved one instead of Weezer covering Toto. If things weren't clicking to begin with, then go ahead and manufacture an excuse about getting up early in the morning or actually being married to a jealous psychopath. But if you like this person, you might take the risk of putting it all out there and explaining exactly why you seemed to completely disappear into yourself halfway through appetizers. They'll almost certainly understand. But if you never hear from them again, remind yourself that you did nothing wrong and take comfort in the fact that it may very well have been some unrelated fatal flaw in your personality or appearance.

They Would've Wanted Me to Orgasm: Sex While Grieving
In some ways, your appetite for food is like your appetite for sex. Your mood plays a role in how much of it you want and how many pancakes are involved. And grief can tamper with your sex drive like little else. On one hand, your libido may have all but vanished, your genitals seeming as vestigial and functionless as your appendix or second eye; on the other hand, all the stress you've been experiencing might manifest itself as surplus sexual energy, a counterintuitive response to grief that Freud characterized as the "Hades boner" after the Greek deity of death and his grim erection. And this can be especially troublesome to the person experiencing it, who may feel guilty for purchasing an

airplane hangar in order to store a pornography supercomputer. So how can people in each group adjust?

If your desire for sex is low, know that it will almost certainly replenish over time, and you'll eventually be able to fully immerse yourself in sex without suddenly second-guessing your decision to forgo a standard casket for the discounted Deli-Paper Special. But it's possible that your inability to sexually function persists, no matter how many weeks pass or how much "passion root" you buy from an online herbalist who probably just sold you fentanyl anyway. That may be because you're resisting memories of your loved one when you should be *integrating* them. When you struggle with arousal, try to imagine your departed loved one right there in the room with you, perhaps seated at the foot of the bed, kneeling on a nearby throw pillow, or, if that seems a bit intrusive, then just watching over you from the doorway. You don't even have to tell your partner, though you might let them know after the fact that your favorite aunt was smiling at you both the whole time and that it made all the difference.

If your sex drive is in overdrive, however, you need to allow yourself those urges without remorse (except the stuff that was nauseating *long* before your loved one passed). Your revved-up libido isn't a betrayal of your grief but a symptom of it, so try swapping your shame for gentle mindfulness. For example, if you have to duck out of a meeting a dozen times to masturbate in a restroom stall, take a moment before each session to declare aloud, "What I do now is the pain in my heart crying out through my hand." An important step in your healing journey is reminding yourself that you're in no way dishonoring the memory of your loved one by working a ten-inch dildo down to the nub.

Breaking the News to Planet Fitness: Your Postmortem Notification Checklist *

People aren't the only ones we have to inform about our loved one's passing. By the time we expire, even if we're young and die on spring break face-down in a kiddie pool filled with coco loco and lube, we're still deeply embedded in the larger bureaucratic and capitalistic culture. And that can be a drag, if for no other reason than no one wants to receive an offer in the mail addressed to a spouse who is now officially beyond considering the Discover card. So once you've told family and friends your loved one has died, which other people and unfeeling entities should you notify?

- Social Security Administration
- Life insurance companies
- Cult home office
- Banks
- Self-Harming Former Child Actors in Recovery support group
- Email providers
- Gym that's going to need to see the original death certificate and a video testimonial from the county coroner in order to even consider not auto-charging the next monthly membership fee, and, even then, it'll take five additional billing cycles to actually go into effect

- Social media sites
- DMV
- Credit card companies
- Quasi-racist social clubs
- Explicitly racist social clubs
- Credit agencies
- "Seventy and Sensual" meetup administrator
- Utility companies, including Internet providers
- Mysterious man who appears in a photo you found in the back of your loved one's wallet and that you're going to assume is your actual biological father
- Streaming entertainment services, such as Netflix and Hulu

* Sincerity Corner: The little things are, of course, always bigger than you think. My mother watched her soaps online, and the simple act of cancelling her account felt like an act of unbearable erasure. I've left her Twitter feed up, however, because I like knowing it's there. It was also pretty much dormant to begin with, consisting as it did of just three tweets all sent out the same day: "Hi," "How are you," and "Jason Roeder."

Grief Journal Prompts

1. "I can count on these people in my support system:
    _____."

    "These people mean well but will ultimately fail me:
    _____."

    "I will rip open the earth and watch smiling as the following
    people drop into the fiery guts of the world: _____."

2. You're considering seeing a grief counselor when you stumble
    across an ad for one on the inside of a yogurt lid. The ad
    appears to be written by hand. Would you call? What ques-
    tions might you ask?

3. "If I ever feel blue at work, I can always confide in _____."
    (Circle at least two.)
    > Stan
    > Marie
    > Donna

4. If you're suddenly triggered on a dinner date, you might
    excuse yourself and hide for a few minutes in the kitchen's
    walk-in freezer. But what might you do if the restaurant stores
    meat unsafely and does not have one?

CHAPTER IV

SELF-CARE: YOU'VE EARNED IT FOR ONCE

But for all the help other people might provide as you grieve, most will have the unmitigated gall to get on with their lives. It might feel strange to witness this. Your very good friend, who's been as supportive as possible, is nevertheless back on social media posting videos of wiener dogs interacting cordially with tortoises. And you're still all gnarly inside. So, in order to sustain your healing, you're going to have to call upon the person who on the most ambitious day of their life might be the laziest person you've ever met, the person you're often astonished is entrusted with any task at all in the world of adults. The person you just know isn't quite right, obviously created by one of God's least reliable subcontractors. That person, of course, is you.

And the self-care you'll require is going to be much more than the spa weekend you rewarded yourself with for some, let's be real, not-that-worthy accomplishment. Restoring yourself is a full-on collaboration of mind and body working together like the sides of a crawdaddy pincer. You'll also likely face the added frustration of not even knowing exactly what you need or when. Or the stubborn conviction that nothing works at all, that maybe it's best if your sadness just dissolves you from the inside-out, and you gently, wetly seep away into your couch cushions. That's all terrifying and normal. But, for now, what are some general principles of self-care?

1. No. You might be familiar with this word from your attempts to get an attractive person's phone number or enroll your four-year-old, who eats pencil shavings, in an elite private kindergarten, but the word *no* also has a function in self-care. It represents the importance of boundaries, of recognizing what you can and simply cannot handle at this time. This is an anxious period in your life, and you're absolutely entitled to opt out. When you've healed, then you can resume saying yes or just continue saying no for the weird or petty reasons you did previously.

2. Lowered Expectations. While you might be getting by, chances are you're doing it irritably or distractedly. Sure, you're back at work, but you've been staring blankly at the same spreadsheet for weeks or just watching as unopened taunts from that serial killer pile up on your desk at the precinct. Part of self-care is acknowledging that in between devastated and recovered (to the extent you will be) is a massive expanse of uneven terrain and that you'll inevitably be resuming your life before you're a hundred percent prepared to do so.

3. Limits of Self-Care. Sure, you got that tattoo lasered off, but the impression will remain. Many decades from now, a nurse's aide will be giving you some kind of antiseptic scrubbing she couldn't possibly be compensated enough for and will notice a faint blemish in the shape of a marijuana leaf surmounting the words, "One Luv." Grief leaves a mark too, even after much time has passed. And all the self-care in the world does not simply erase it.

I THINK, THEREFORE I'M CRYING IN THIS HONDA DEALERSHIP: TENDING TO YOUR GRIEVING MIND

The average human brain weighs about three pounds, fully nude. But when you're grieving, it can feel like so much more. Despite it having been so reliable for storing names, doubting God, and reminding you that your shellfish allergy is going to end you if you so much as touch that crab cake, it can seem like your brain just isn't up to the task right now. If you could just step out of your feelings for a few minutes the way strippers step out of their clothes for the duration of The Pussycat Dolls' "Don't Cha," maybe you'd be all right. But one of the first and hardest lessons that we learn when we lose someone is that it is nothing at all like "Don't Cha." To the extent that grief comes and goes, it does so on its own terms. Maybe if you examine it, however, you can be better prepared for it when it shows up.

It's Happening Again: Triggers
When you object to something cruel a comedian says about a person or group who has nowhere near the platform to respond in kind, you might be accused of being "triggered," a well-earned putdown for your limp-dick compassion for others. But then there are grief triggers, stimuli that really flip your misery switch. Sometimes it's easy to anticipate them: an old birthday card you've saved from your mother, a video of your father drunkenly putting Elastigirl in a full nelson at Disney World. But it's not always so predictable. Often we don't know why something is setting us off, why a commercial for Dentyne Ice has suddenly and irrevocably ruined our day. And then there are times we don't even know *what* is setting us off in the first place, let alone its specific significance. All we know is that one minute we're collected, if not necessarily fine, and the next it's like we're back at the funeral watching the priest get our loved one's name and gender wrong. But while grief can approach almost silently—there's a reason most therapists refer to it as the Doleful Prius—you can at least get caught off-guard less often by cultivating an awareness of it.

The concept of mindfulness may have acquired a slight New Age aftertaste in recent years. Nothing disqualifying, just kind of how fast-food burgers have the faintest suggestion of the suppressive chemical used to keep them from coming to life. But mindfulness is actually pretty straightforward. It's paying attention and paying attention *to* your paying attention. By attending to your thoughts when you find yourself triggered, by striving to be present in that moment, you can learn to identify what's agitating you and begin to slow it all down.

For example, let's say you're at CVS. Congratulations! It's another glorious afternoon in the eye care and oral hygiene aisle. Suddenly, a wave of sadness and anxiety washes over you. Try taking deep breaths. Focus on something physical in your environment to ground you—an item on the shelf, even your own foot. Be present. When you've gathered yourself, try taking an inventory of your surroundings and your thoughts. What was it that might have brought these emotions on? Maybe it had nothing to do with grief. Maybe your long-repressed memory of the time you were manhandled by security for stuffing fifty tubes of cold-sore ointment down your pants has suddenly reemerged. Or maybe your grief has made an unconscious but overwhelming connection with something in your environment. What might that be? Maybe you realize that the speakers overhead are playing the same Fine Young Cannibals song your grandmother used to sing to you when you were little, or perhaps that bottle of contact lens solution in front of you is very similar to the one your father got you for your high-school graduation present. When you know these things, you can know what to avoid, or at least approach with greater understanding. It takes practice, however. And not everything is going to have a tidy cause and effect in the first place—many times, in fact, the sadness inside just sloshes to the surface wherever and whenever, as impossible to predict as the weather or the phases of the moon.*

Unleashing the Power of Sentences: Grief Affirmations
Affirmations may seem pointless and ridiculous. For one thing, why would you listen to someone such as yourself? You've had a frosted-tip mullet, earnestly told friends to take their baby to a chiropractor, and willingly paid hundreds more in rent for a view the realtor openly called an "active vermin battleground." And, for another, if affirmations aren't quite full-on woo-woo, they can certainly be mistaken for it at a distance if they're wearing similar pants. But when you think about it, there is a logic to them. Even when we're not grieving, many of us constantly send ourselves discouraging messages, little brutal telegrams from our subconscious that we can't hear but that we internalize over and over every day.

TELEGRAM

INTELLIGENCE AND PHYSICAL APPEAL MINIMAL WITH LITTLE PROMISE FOR IMPROVEMENT -(STOP)- ADDITIONAL FLAWS ENUMERATED SOON IN FUTURE COMMUNICATIONS - (STOP)- POOR SOCIAL SKILLS AND DISCOLORATION OF TEETH TO BE EMPHASIZED -(STOP)-

---

* **Sincerity Corner:** I don't have any specific triggers. Sure, that first Mother's Day was a drag, and I'm definitely not wild about the fact she'll never call me on my birthday to tell me the story of my prenatal largeness and the specialist who had to be summoned to rotate me because I was sideways in her poor womb. It's more like, every now and then, a day or even an hour just feels a little heavier, and that's probably never changing.

And when you are grieving, those subliminal bulletins can just rain down on you even more often than they usually do and with even more ferocity.

TELEGRAM

```
NEVER HAPPY AGAIN NEVER HAPPY AGAIN NEVER HAPPY
AGAIN NEVER HAPPY AGAIN NEVER HAPPY AGAIN NEVER
HAPPY AGAIN NEVER HAPPY AGAIN NEVER HAPPY AGAIN
-(STOP)-
```

Affirmations, then, are just little bits of deliberate counterprogramming designed to provide you with at least an alternative to bottomless misery. You can write them down or speak them aloud, in private or during work meetings when Bryan from marketing is taking his sweet time showing up. Or you can just think them with a ferocious intensity that makes your forehead boil and your eyebrows evaporate right off. However you deliver them to yourself, it's important to select the right ones, because the last thing you need are affirmations that actually work against you.

"My grief will conquer me by Thursday, latest."

"I am a mushroom, and grief is the unrelenting truffle hog that will root me out of the earth."

While you'll have to put a little time into crafting affirmations that address how you're specifically suffering, consider using the following as jumping-off points that you can modify as you need.

"I may not be stronger than my grief, but I will definitely bore it to death."

"My grief will not be my prison, or, if anything, it will be one of those rehabilitation-focused prisons they have in Norway which are more like dormitories and which teach you how to groom horses."

"There is enough strength in me to fill a half-gallon orange juice container."

"I am a Toyota Corolla floor mat.

My pain is the dirt and crumbs that cling to my fabric.

The Compassionate Universe shakes me out at the vacuum kiosk of the self-serve car wash and releases my pain as dust that coats a nearby, freshly waxed F-150 whose bumper sticker reads 'It's OK To Be White.'

I will be whole again."*

Thanks but More Thanks: Gratitude in Grief

John Merrick, aka the "Elephant Man," famously wrote in his diary, "I have been disfigured and despised all of my life; but that the sun still shines upon a face such as mine is attestation that I am blessed and favoured by God as any of His other children." He actually never wrote that—he died tragically while sleeping at age twenty-seven from the weight of his own head—but what's more important than the verity of the quotation is its deeper takeaway: gratitude can be found even under the most unlikely circumstances, and that also includes the death of someone we love.

If we're being honest, however, most of us don't feel gratitude

---

* **Sincerity Corner:** Honestly, just try telling yourself that you're fine every now and then. You'd be amazed at how far that can go toward making you believe it. I have told myself, like, with actual spoken words, "You're OK," on a number of occasions. It doesn't stick forever, of course, but it tweaks my mood in a way that really surprises me.

as often or as powerfully as we should. Sure, we mutter a hurried "thanks" when the cashier drops the receipt in the bag or the firefighter hands us our baby intact, but all that is just learned courtesy. The time we spend truly reflecting on the privileges of our life is minimal; in fact, in most rankings, it's one of the things we spend the least amount of time doing per year.

Rank

996. Seeing if eating slice of pizza upside down tastes different

997. Reopening official inquiry into disappearance of Amelia Earhart

998. Gratitude

999. Checking fingers again to make sure any cool double-jointed ones didn't slip under radar

Although grief hardly feels like an occasion for gratitude—where do you send your thank-you bear to multiple organ failure?—it can be. You're grieving because you had an attachment that was meaningful, even wonderful, which was a gift in a universe that generally speaking isn't all that invested in your happiness. Contemplating this may seem like the limpest consolation since, "Someone in Russia stole my identity, which is great because I always wanted to travel abroad," but it may be helpful. Some people cultivate gratitude in writing as a way of focusing on what they have and not what they've lost. Maybe they start each day with a list of five random things to be thankful for, or have a template that they turn to each time, something like:

Something that made me smile in the past twenty-four hours is _____.

Aside from the serpent-shaped birthmark the Vatican is currently investigating, one thing that makes me special is _____.

I am grateful to not currently reside in this notorious POW camp: _____.

A delicious meal I once enjoyed despite the fact I'd been tricked into eating an endangered species was _____.

When I'm feeling blue, I always know I can listen to _____ and their smash 1978 self-titled debut.

YOUR FLAB'S BITTER TEARS:
TENDING TO YOUR GRIEVING BODY

We certainly talk a big game about physical fitness in this country. We've got all kinds of gyms and yoga studios and CrossFit dungeons, not to mention workout apps and wearable trackers that gently drill into our wrist bones when we haven't met our daily step quota. But if you're like most Americans, you aren't nearly as obsessed with physical fitness as you have the opportunity to be—that Peloton's just sitting there waiting for spiders to figure out what to do with it while you have brisket smokers running in every room of your house. And when you're grieving, the bad can easily slip into worse.

Of course, this is a trying time, and you may be experiencing a hormonal mayhem of the sort you haven't had since you were an adolescent and constantly rubbing up against a pillow or shellshocked plushie. But as difficult as it may seem, you'll be better off if you tend to your flesh, even a little.

Try Eating Well. There may be days now and then where you'll want

Overlooked Meditation Apps

You can think of meditation as a kind of homework, except it's mindfulness practice and you can't copy off the kid you think is smart but find out too late is just kind of shrunken and weird. Through meditation, you can learn not to defeat your grief, but to coexist with it, to observe it impassively instead of being repeatedly mule-kicked by it. And these days, we get our guided meditations the same way we get our food and the significant other we'll eventually have to lock out of the house: apps. Headspace and Calm are two of the most popular, but there are other under-the-radar options with unique features.

How Far Did I Meditate?

For fitness enthusiasts, this app monitors the distance traveled during each meditation practice, in amounts as little as half an inch for slight scootching and up to a maximum of twelve feet for getting up and sticking the cat in another room.

Iron Serenity

You can't spell "worm" without "om." Submissives need not sacrifice the cruelty they have so richly earned in order to enjoy the benefits of meditation. Each guided practice features narration from a certified meditation instructor and agony goddess who will allow you to breathe deeply only when it pleases her.

Zen Choppers

If you're among the many people who just can't immerse themselves in a guided meditation unless it's conducted by someone with loose dentures, you're in luck. The practices on this app, ranging from five minutes to an hour, are narrated entirely by instructors with false teeth that clatter, slurp, and occasionally fall out completely onto the microphone.

Giving Lotus

Even though the time you put into meditation will ultimately benefit others, some people still feel guilty about "navel gazing." But not with this app, in which every practice you successfully complete donates one toy to a local shelter for women and children, and every practice you fail to complete removes one.

to demolish a footlong meatball parm and an entire chocolate marble bread before wolfing down two full pounds of Thanksgiving sides as a nightcap. On the other hand, you might not have much of an appetite at all. Food is stupid and needs to shut up. But good nutrition, including lean proteins, fruits, vegetables—you know, all the stuff that makes eating a chore—can help boost your mood so that even your bad days aren't necessarily devastating ones. Monitoring your hydration is essential too. You might be distracted and not even think about having a glass of water until you're already tired or a tiny sand dune appears on your tongue.

Move Your Body. Physical activity ramps up production of chemicals in your brain that reduce stress. And it doesn't have to be some manic cardio jag that leaves you gasping on the floor of an elliptical room and covered in little hand towels by embarrassed gym staff. Just going for a casual walk around the block can be beneficial, not to mention spare onlookers the psychological injury of beholding your sweaty body. And if nature, to you, isn't just a filthy place where mosquito bites, bird shit, and drowning live, you can upgrade that walk into a hike. Whatever you do, at least try to do it a little every day. If you're struggling, shame one of your more deferential friends into keeping you motivated by participating with you. If they're at all reluctant, all you have to do is smile faintly and say, "That's OK, buddy. Maybe I'll just stay home. The drawn curtains, stale air, and time all alone with my agony will probably do me a world of good."

Get Some Sleep.* "Wildly erratic" isn't just what your boss wrote

---

* **Sincerity Corner:** I was sleeping so poorly while my mother was in the hospital that the only thing that kept me from driving off the road was coffee and sheer embarrassment at the thought of being wheeled past my family on a gurney to the ICU room next to hers.

about your job performance or commitment to wearing deodorant. It probably describes your grieving sleeping pattern, and there's a reasonable chance you were already one of the many Americans who can't sleep without a forty-five-minute ASMR video of marbles being gently dropped on Jell-O. Or, if you're not tossing and turning all night, you might be sleeping too much, rousing yourself from bed in the afternoon and only because your hungry dog was legit tearing at your calf muscle. When you're grieving, it can seem like normalcy is gone for good, and while you might distract yourself in daylight hours, depression, anger, and anxiety will be your flight crew for your long overnight trip. But there are some steps you can take.

- Make sure your room is cool and dark. Sleep experts suggest your room should feel like being locked in the trunk of a car that's parked outside on a crisp autumn day.

- Stop using devices such as phones or laptops about an hour before you go to bed, and store them where you can't easily access them, like across the room or at the center of an intricate maze.

- Keep naps short. When you shut your eyes, explain to the dream-manufacturing region of your subconscious that you're just popping in for a quick sec, so it doesn't need to waste its time having your third-grade teacher burst from a cocoon.

- Studies suggest massage releases hormones that aid in relax-ation, so ask the exercise buddy I mentioned above if they wouldn't also mind giving you a full-body jojoba oil rubdown.

The Grief Calorie Counter

Most doctors describe the human body as a furnace with strategically placed body hair. That's because everything we do—walking, sleeping, even competing in the Tour de France—burns calories to generate energy. And grief is no exception. It's not exactly a kettlebell circuit, but if you're watching your weight, every little bit helps.

Activity	Calories Burned/Hour
Just lying there	30
Just standing there	40
Crying (suppressed)	55
Crying (standard)	65
Crying (heaving)	75
Aggressively snuggling pet	55
Returning funeral shoes to Marshalls	90
Rapidly aborted yoga sequence	05
Call with loved one, comforting	60
Call with loved one, accusatory	180
Scrubbing floors until house foundation visible	1,500

Just Manage the Alcohol and Drugs. Try to get through this without having a species of opium poppy named after you, that's all.

NO ONE'S GONNA HAVE THE BALLS TO TELL YOU YOUR POEM SUCKS: CREATING YOUR WAY THROUGH GRIEF

OK, maybe you're not a creative person. Maybe you once had a creative impulse, but it vanished the day you showed your parents a picture you drew at school and they immediately called an ambulance. Maybe a quilt fragment is still stitched to your stomach from that one time you tried to use a sewing machine. But you might find that expressing yourself, even if it's just *to* yourself, is beneficial as you work through your grief. It doesn't have to be a masterpiece. Odds are, whatever you produce is going to be something a fourth grader would do and a fifth grader would redo, so just focus on what you might get out of it. The good news is that there are as many ways to create as there are cans of paint or words in the dictionary. Let's just assume that's four.

A Grief Journal. The journal prompts at the end of each chapter have hopefully enabled you to process your thoughts and feelings more productively and attractively than if you'd just been left to your own devices. Still, if you're able, there's also a potential emotional release in sitting down without any cues and writing anything that comes to mind, just letting it all storm onto the page like a melancholy bison stampede. You might be amazed at what insights emerge when you're not really trying, and since when have you missed an opportunity to avoid effort?

Letters to Your Deceased Loved One. If writing in a journal feels as awkward as cooking dinner with your feet, then this will feel as awkward as eating that dinner. But writing a letter can be an opportunity to tell someone things you couldn't bring yourself to tell them in life, good and bad, and to stay connected by updating them on events they are now spared from witnessing personally. Your letters can be long and impassioned or respectful and to the point.

Father:

I hope this letter finds you well. I am thriving at work, and my newborn baby has your jaundiced complexion. However, we believe hers is temporary.

I love you and resent you in equal proportion.

Warmly,

Jennifer

And when you're done, you can tear it up, seal it in an envelope, and keep it with you, or ritually burn it, imagining your message rising upward and setting off all the smoke alarms in Heaven.

Spelling out 'Come Back, Mommy' with Christmas lights on your roof might not be your neighbors' idea of art, but it doesn't have to be.

Arts and Crafts. Whether it's a pietà of the Virgin Mary cradling dead Jesus in her arms or fan art of a nude woman riding Larry Flynt's erupting zombie boner through the earth in front of his tombstone, the visual arts have long been used as a medium for expressing grief. You can meticulously draft a photorealistic portrait of your loved one or draw a more charitable likeness that omits the five-inch facial scar they received thirty-five years ago while fighting over a Cabbage Patch Kid. You can just let your emotions guide your hand as you daub splotches of paint on a canvas or make a collage out of seashells and discarded e-cig cartridges you found at your loved one's favorite beach— whatever you end up doing is what you needed to do. And when you're done, you might share your work with others suffering from the same loss. Maybe they themselves didn't convert an abandoned herbicide factory into an installation called the Museum of Dad, but they can at least participate in your vision from a place of love and recognition.

A Grief Playlist. If you can torture just a few rudimentary chords out of an instrument, you can use it to deal with your grief. But if you're someone who gave up music because practicing was tedious or the instructor at Guitar Center clearly began reassessing everything about their job before you got three measures into "Suck My Kiss," there's another option: a grief playlist. With streaming services like Spotify, you can gather up songs that bind you to your loved one because they were among his or her favorites in life or that just put you in a tender but non-devastated headspace. Be sure to burn a copy onto a CD for those occasions where you find yourself in a twenty-four-year-old rental car.

Eleven Little Ways to Brighten Your Day

Grief therapists often say that just as a few drops of venomous king cobra spit can kill an elephant, healing can come in tiny doses too. You'd be surprised at how small indulgences and adventures like the ones below can help get you through your darkest hours.

Visit the wine shop and splurge on a bottle without a picture of a chateau covered in a fumigation tent.

Be a dish for the night! Take a Lemon Joy bubble bath.

Order a pizza, and when the driver arrives, talk like a pirate or just listen like one.

Watch forty-second pornography snippets in a tuxedo or ballgown.

Bring a parrot to the dog park and then ask everyone there how their dogs got so weird and fucked-up looking.

Climb onto your roof at dawn and pretend you're making the sun rise with a magical flute.

How about a random act of kindness? Tell the barista that, in addition to your coffee, you want the person behind you to buy his.

Take Gordon Ramsay's *MasterClass* and then hound him till he makes you executive sous chef.

Catch up with an old friend from high school and find out which ethnic group she thinks is pulling the government's strings these days.

Throw a dart at a map of your house and travel to whatever room it lands on.

Give yourself a big ol' hug but not a bigger hug than the one you know you truly deserve.

Grief Journal Prompts

1. Write down three things you did to take care of yourself today. You can include things you forced servants to do: _____, _____, _____.

2. When was the last time you were triggered? Focus on events related to grief and not your preexisting frailty.

3. How much of your diet now consists of lean protein and vegetables vs. stuffed-crust pizza wrapped in sheets of bacon and saturated in three kinds of drippings?

4. Imagine you're sending your loved one a postcard from Disney World. What would you tell them about your trip, and how might you complain to them about persons in wheelchairs getting on rides first?

CHAPTER V

KEEPING THEM ALIVE, THOUGH NOT REALLY

When a person we care about dies, we don't just wipe our hands and say, "Well, guess they're annihilated." It's only natural to want to preserve their memory, not in a sacrilegious or "Buddy, you'd be better off not looking in that closet" way, but in such a way that the connection with our loved one stays intact. We can summon a memory of them whenever we want to be comforted, inspired, or not-so-subtly condemned for our interracial relationship. We can broadly keep them alive in how we treat other people and ourselves. But there are also all kinds of smaller, specific gestures too. Maybe we wear a ring they once wore or make a onetime five-dollar donation to a charitable cause that was precious to them—with some imagination there's always a way to keep the one we lost a little closer to us and a little further away from Heaven.

As you prepare to memorialize your loved one, think about who they were in life and whether they'd really want to keep the association with you going after their death. If not, no biggie. You can just use the photo compartment of your locket for a picture of your beloved pet or favorite pizza. But if so, consider how they would want to be honored. Maybe they enjoyed nature or actively participated in the community. Maybe they loved football* or were just a fan of structured brutality in general. Once you understand the *who*, the *how* opens up wide, and

---

* **Sincerity Corner:** The extent of my mother's involvement in football was occasionally looking up from her clipboard (nursing also came with hours of paperwork at home) if I happened to be watching the Dolphins game. She wasn't really emotionally invested, though she would suffer through a little moment of devastation when a kicker, on either team, missed a field goal. She hoped he and his teammates would still be friends.

all kinds of possibilities present themselves.

Or you can just keep a couple pounds of them in a jar.

ASHES: THE RESIDUE OF LOSS

Did you know that until 2017 it was perfectly legal in every state to store the corpse of a deceased family member at home as long as it wasn't posed provocatively in a street-facing window? Except in Florida, where doing so was mandatory? While that's not the kind of thing most of us would be into, some people still want to have a little morsel of their loved one in their possession, kind of as a way of telling death it missed a spot. Often it means storing in an urn what we assume are our loved one's reverently cremated remains and not a heaping scoop from a pail labeled "Jumbled Bone Specks." We can then display that urn in a place of honor, like the mantel or a shelf in an entertainment unit next to an old DVD of *Rounders*. And since that vessel is now essentially our loved one's new body from now until we pick the worst possible place to practice our gymnastics routine, it's important to know how to choose the right one.

First, make sure your urn is the right size for the body weight of your loved one. Too small, and you may end up having to purchase an additional urn sidecar for the spillover. Better to err on the side of a slightly larger urn and just tell people that your loved one insisted on being cremated with their beloved moose.

Urns come in many different materials—ceramic, wood, and porcelain, just to name a few—so think not only about what's most attractive but also what's most durable in a given environment. For example, you might want to avoid a metal urn that will rust in the rain if you're also using it to plug a hole in your roof. Meanwhile, a fragile glass urn might be a poor choice if you have small children and they haven't yet learned that your gun is way more interesting.

You don't need to embellish the urn. Maybe your loved one was a no-frills kind of person who already would've been scandalized by the fact that you didn't store their ashes in a rinsed-out soup can with their name scrawled in marker over the word "Progresso." But if you do decide to customize, you've got options. Engravings can turn a boring, tasteful urn into a tribute to your loved one's favorite hobby, animal, or cartel affiliation. You can also get their very own likeness laser etched into the urn, which can act as a helpful reminder for whenever you forget exactly who it was you pretty much poured into a vase.

Sometimes the urn is the whole story. The ashes are deposited into the urn, and the family then places it in a reasonably dignified location at home beneath subtle accent lighting and a few feet from the worst of any known infestations. But sometimes a portion or even all of the cremated remains, or "cremains" if you're looking to squeeze it into a newspaper's personal ad, go off on a scattering adventure at a place your loved one cherished. Maybe it's the ocean if they loved boating or the woods if they loved wood. An aerial scattering might be perfect for someone who was a fan of planes but was too chicken in life to be launched from a 747 without a parachute. Rules for scattering vary, especially on private property, so be sure to conduct due diligence, or sit there helplessly while an irate squad of Disney custodians power-washes your loved one off the walls of Cinderella's castle.

Finally, if storing or scattering your loved one's actual ashes just feels a little too gritty for your liking, there are now ways to incorporate them into the very substance of another object—everything from jewelry and artwork to ink or even an actual playing record. If you're making the decision, you probably know your loved one better than most and can best determine how they'd feel about spending eternity as a paperweight or pile of beads.

OTHER BODILY SOUVENIRS

Maybe your loved one wasn't cremated. Perhaps they had a religious objection or worried it would hurt their chances of being allowed to join an undead army. But just because you don't have ashes to work with doesn't mean you can't take a little bit of your loved one to go.

Locks of Hair. A little snip off the top can be made into jewelry, glued into a scrapbook, or even framed. While it's standard practice to cut off just a tiny piece of hair, on rare occasion much larger quantities are taken and made into hang gliders or baseball-field tarps.

Tattoos. Believe it or not, skin art can be lasered off, preserved, and framed so that you never forget how much your loved one liked dragons or misattributed Marilyn Monroe quotes. Before getting one of these keepsakes, however, ask yourself if "$EXY BEA$T" really needs a second go-round in the world of the living.

Unattractive Features. If you're considering laying your loved one to rest in one of those cemeteries in Los Angeles that caters to beautiful people, you may want to or even be forced to remove unsightly anatomy, such as a larger-than-average nose or abhorrently visible ears. While such cemeteries will rarely accept bodies that aren't perfect, they have occasionally been known to make an exception for those they consider obese but will look fine as hell once they decompose about fifty pounds.

Everything You Can Grab in Sixty Seconds. While so-called "body booths" have been banned pretty much everywhere at this point, some old-school funeral directors aren't beyond a little fun and will let you take home as much of your loved one as you can stuff in your pockets in under a minute.

DEATH 4 CASH: MEMORIAL CHARITABLE WORKS

If your prosperous career or success filing nuisance lawsuits has left you with a little disposable income, you can put it toward a noble cause as a tribute to your loved one. This can be straightforward if there was a nonprofit or some other do-gooder entity they were dedicated to in life. It'd frankly be weird to not kick in a few bucks on behalf of someone who had a Human Rights Watch–themed wedding. Or perhaps a contribution reflecting the nature of their passing. Maybe a gift to the American Heart Association if they died from heart disease or to an anti-circumcision group if they died from low foreskin count. No matter how vanishingly little of your inheritance you'd like to spend on this, there's always a way to pay it forward.

Direct Charitable Gifts. It's worth adding that, while you might have the impulse to make a gift in your loved one's name, you might not know exactly where. Maybe the only charitable work they themselves performed in life was dropping off a single, densely soiled loveseat cushion outside a Goodwill. And maybe they never expressed strong opinions about helping others, tersely muttering, "No comment," when asked their opinion about pediatric cancer research. Without obvious charitable leanings, you may have to step back and think about who they were and what they valued. If they loved animals, maybe a gift to an animal advocacy group or local shelter; if they didn't, maybe a gift to a nearby poultry processing facility. Did they like football so much that they sent your college fund to the Dallas Cowboys to help

A Short History of Urns, the World's First Containers

Cremation originated thousands of years ago, both as a funereal practice and a sport—fossil evidence suggests that many millennia before the first Olympic Games, intertribal competitions were held to determine who could burn the most fresh corpses in the time it took for the sun to rise over the horizon or for a baby snake to fully emerge from an egg. But while cremation can be traced almost as far back as the discovery of fire itself, the advent of vessels to store the ashes in surprisingly came much later.

Early container technology was so primitive as to be useless. The archaeological record is filled with ancient efforts to store water in a spiderweb or grain in the gentle scoop of a dry, fallen leaf. That's why, when a body was cremated, family members would try to take home what ashes they could in their hands and piled on top of their heads. But almost all of it would fall off in transit. Meanwhile, the larger amount which could not be carried was simply allowed to be dispersed in the wind, washed away in the rain, or naturally assimilated into anthills. It was so devastating to surrender a loved one's remains to the elements that the practice of cremation itself began to fall out of favor. Why go to all the trouble of cremating a dead loved one if there was no way to hold onto even a few precious scoops of them?

The unsung hero in the history of urns, and indeed containers more generally, is a poor farmer estimated to have lived around 2000 BCE in what is now modern Turkmenistan. After the cremation of his father, he is believed to have discovered the man's skull not only mostly intact but also filled with a generous helping of his own incinerated brains. Holding it in his hands, he was delighted by how secure it was, how little spilled beyond a few grains, here and there, from the eye sockets. He didn't realize it at the time, and never would—dying as he did soon after from generalized peasant maladies—but he had singlehandedly saved cremation and invented the first urn.

This urn became the model for all the glass jars, ceramic vases, and bronze jugs to follow. It seemed so obvious in hindsight that most historians will just come out and say how deeply embarrassed they are for these people. But skulls continued to be used as urns for thousands of additional years, maybe for sentimental reasons or the undeniable convenience. The historical record is unclear on when the skull urn finally fell out of favor and if it ever did so completely. In fact, if you ask your funeral home director if they have a skull urn, they'll definitely say no. However, there's still a chance they'll pause, lower their voice, and say, "But what if I did?"

them hold onto a couple of quality free agents? Well, lots of teams and individual players have charitable affiliations. Once you've figured out what they loved, the rest is so much easier. Where there's a will, there's an organization with its hand out that's going to squander most of your gift on administrative costs anyway.

Scholarships. What could be more noble than igniting, or partially igniting if your gift's not realistically going to cover more than books, the higher-education career of a college student? Year after year, a scholarship with your loved one's name attached to it can help a budding scholar focus more on their studies than the menial or erotic services they'd otherwise be providing to pay for them. A scholarship can also be a way of supporting your loved one's alma mater or their former field of study, assuming they pursued business administration because they wanted to and not because it was the only major their domineering father didn't dismiss as useless, socialist, or strictly for gays.

Public Memorials. A public memorial is a great way to situate your tribute in a place in the world that was special to your loved one. Maybe it's a plaque defacing a boulder along a hiking trail they enjoyed or mounted on a park bench at the very spot they spent hours on end surreptitiously tripping joggers. Stadiums, playgrounds, and theaters are just a few of the spots where you can dedicate a visible chunk of surface area, not to mention the fact that your memorial can take the form of a public event. Celebrate your loved one by sponsoring a free showing of their favorite film or a concert in the park that treats the whole community to the symphonic interpretation of Sammy Hagar they never knew they needed.

Starting a Nonprofit to Undermine a Nonprofit Which You Irrationally Believe Wronged Your Loved One. Maybe you wouldn't be grieving right now if the almighty American Lung Association had stepped the fuck up and found a cure for chronic obstructive pulmonary disease. If, in your grief, you're prone to wholly unreasonable outbursts such as this, you might consider starting up a competing nonprofit to siphon off precious resources and ultimately bring the rival organization to its knees.

Just Destroying It. Maybe your loved one, far from really being invested in anything in the world, was fond of tenderly saying, "The one truth is the meaninglessness of truth. I neither care nor don't care that I ever met you or that either of us is here right now. My relationship to everything is nothing. I am pure self-negation. I am the dinosaurs as well as the asteroid that wiped them out. Or none of these things." In cases where your loved one cultivated a lifelong alienation from existence itself, consider just burning or shredding the money in honor of there being literally nothing worth doing with it. It's exactly the kind of nihilistic tribute they wouldn't care if you did or not.

GAME NIGHT GOT WEIRD: NEW AND OLD TRADITIONS

Whether it's carving pumpkins for Halloween or indulging libertarians over a Thanksgiving feast, traditions are crucial for reinforcing the bonds between family and friends. After all, traditions aren't just generic activities themselves—my springtime maypole frolic may look nothing like yours—they're rituals that tend to revolve around a core cast of characters. When one of them dies, it can be difficult to know what to do with the tradition they made feel so essential. But the truth is that the tradition *exactly* as you knew it is already gone, so you couldn't truly continue even if you tried. You could plan your Fourth of July barbecue just as you always do, but without your grill master and their annual skin graft at the burn unit, it's just something else. So is it just best to abandon these traditions altogether?

You have the option, of course, of opting out. If the very thought of watching football on Sunday without your dad by your side to roll his eyes every time one of today's soft players gets a so-called traumatic brain injury, you can feel free to consider the tradition closed. But it doesn't necessarily have to be like that, especially if you know your loved one would be sad to be the reason you're no longer going on your weekend hike or holding your yearly Good Friday Crucifixion Cabaret. You might try incorporating your absent loved one into an existing tradition such that the living can continue to enjoy it while the dead remain tastefully visible. For example, if it's trivia night, you can kick off the quizzing with a question from their favorite category or allow each player to look up an answer on their phone in the guise of texting, like your loved one used to do, thinking no one ever noticed. If it's an Easter egg hunt, you can simply name it after your loved one and explain to the children that having a holiday event named after you is one of the many perks of being dead.

If that seems too forced, you can always inaugurate a brand-new tradition. After all, traditions have to start somewhere. Valentine's Day spontaneously came into existence when confectioners realized they could move more heart candies if they had playful, romantic messages on them instead of just "THIS IS A HEART" or "THIRD INGREDIENT IS DEXTROSE." If your loved one's absence is built into the occasion from the start, you might feel less like you're defiling something sacred. On your deceased father's birthday, for instance, you might get a meal at his favorite Italian restaurant, buy presents he would've loved and then donate them in his honor, or take turns reading aloud from his favorite book on the last days of the Third Reich. You'll know you've created a good memorial tradition when it connects you with your loved one, and you're just a tiny bit glad they're not there to ruin it.

TRAVELING, BUNGEE JUMPING, SMASHING THE BOSS'S WINDSHIELD: COMPLETING YOUR LOVED ONE'S BUCKET LIST

No one wants to die with regrets. Who wants to be lying on their deathbed wishing like hell they'd spent more time with their family or a different, superior family? Who wants that sickening moment of realizing, as the last light fades and the world slowly recedes before their dying eyes, that they might be running out of time to learn alto sax? Some people die knowing full well they squandered the one life they were blessed with and that maybe it should've gone to someone else or been distributed among fifteen or so adorable cats. But even people who lived passionately and productively leave the world with at least a little unfinished business—some project, adventure, or sexual insertion ritual that went unfulfilled. And that's where you come in. You can finish their bucket list.

If you're extraordinarily lucky, they have an official list put down on paper, most really formidable entries crossed out, and just a couple of ridiculously simple stragglers remaining—sure, you'll buy a plant and visit a Burger King. But your loved one may very well have a whole docket of big-time challenges with barely anything accomplished. You could spend the rest of your own life doing everything they failed to do in theirs. At this point, it becomes a matter of prioritizing, doing just enough to satisfy the spirit of the list with a series of somewhat less ambitious alternate experiences. Let me show you what I mean.

Intended Experience	Alternate Experience
Go to Mardi Gras	Fling tequila-soaked beads at FedEx driver
Do one hundred push-ups, good ones	Do five push-ups, assisted by elaborate pulley apparatus
Learn the constellations	Learn moon
Go on safari	Ride scooter down hamster aisle at PetSmart
Go vegetarian for entire month	Eat one less fistful of veal for entire week
Get PhD	Complete three-day bartending intensive
Volunteer at soup kitchen	Lob can of creamy mushroom into homeless encampment
Get crazy tattoo	Draw small flower in pen incorporating existing mole
Do karaoke in front of packed bar	Write down "Bohemian Rhapsody" lyrics, gently lay them on pillow
Take cross-country road trip	Travel as far as medium-sized dog can drag you

Of course, your loved one might not have had a bucket list. Maybe for them, life was about monotony and routine and, if they were feeling wild, tedium. More likely, they just never put their aspirations down on paper. But they probably said something that suggested a goal of some sort, and maybe you can shape that into an all-new bucket list that you then carry out yourself. So think back to conversations you had. It should be obvious what you can do with statements such as these:

• "I always wanted to visit the Grand Canyon."

- "I'd love to go skydiving, but I refuse to do it with any company that doesn't test the parachute on a chimp first."

- "One day, I hope to eat cheese and crackers, not just separately but combined."

- "Before I die, I would like to break Shridhar Chillal's record for the longest fingernails on one hand at a combined 358.1 inches."

- "I just hope I get a chance to buy a nuke on the black market and menace the world with it."*

PLANT A TREE

Even after someone dies, life itself carries on as usual for virtually everyone else. Thousands of people in the world have already gone the way of all flesh by the time we've reached the point in our morning where we're sorting through the options in the muffin case. This is life continuing in the most indifferent way possible. It can be disheartening to know that, on the final day of your loved one's existence, a great many people had nothing more than everyday concerns, such as where they lost their phone or how much to tip the surrogate mother who birthed their twins. But planting a memorial tree is different. When you plant a tree on behalf of your loved one, their

---

* **Sincerity Corner:** Most of the things my mother wanted, that I know of, she wanted for her sons. Aside from general happiness and prosperity, my mother wanted me to appear on *Wheel of Fortune* and to contact Jay Leno directly for writing work. Any time I had a late-night packet rejected, she was wonderful about reminding me that so-and-so was just an asshole anyway.

death becomes the catalyst for new life that wouldn't have otherwise been sticking out of the ground. Whether it's in a majestic national forest or just a local vacant lot where that daycare center that was on the news used to be, a tree is a memorial that can stand as a living tribute, possibly for generations. And with biodegradable urns, you can even incorporate your loved one's ashes into the tree itself, so they'll literally live on in the roots and branches that provide a home for ungrateful birds.

YOU ARE THE MEMORIAL

In the end, your "memorial" may be as simple as allowing your loved one's example to guide you, to gently take control of higher functioning in your brain like an alien parasite that literally nourishes itself on thought. Think of the qualities that made your loved one a person worth grieving for in the first place and not some rando who kind of has your nose but who could burst into flame in front of you and not alter your plans for cosmic bowling. We're not necessarily talking big-ticket triumphs either. It's not about climbing a mountain they climbed or evading an international manhunt they evaded, but maybe just their kindness or generosity. Asking yourself what your loved one would do is a way to keep them alive time and time again—when you check on the elderly neighbor you ordinarily would've left alone until you heard audible groans through the walls, or build a wheelchair for an injured mouse that has no idea what the fuck to do with it, you'll know you're not doing it alone. What could be a better tribute than that?

A Word on Necromancy

You weren't buying that "you are the memorial stuff," were you? In fact, maybe you've determined that everything discussed in this chapter is, well, useless. Spiritually affirming, sure, but a glorified Altoids tin filled with ashes representing 0.0001 percent of your loved one's mass isn't going to cut it. You've admittedly lost your mind a little and want your loved one back—as in, all the way back. "Closure" is for chumps. You're heading for the dark arts, baby, and you're going to turn this death thing right around. I can't endorse this move in a book dedicated to coping with death, not demanding a refund from it. But if you must employ black magic, at least keep a couple of things in mind.

First, don't go it alone. Never jump into necromancy based on a couple of YouTube clips from some sixteen-year-old named NinjaShaman who interrupts his video to thank the manscaping trimmer that sponsored it. That's exactly how novices end up not only failing to bring back their loved one but also in eternal bondage to the Archfiend.

Assuming you contract with an outside sorcerer, don't be shy about asking to verify any pacts they've struck with evil incarnate, and make sure they're up to date. Anyone can advertise that they raise the dead on a website, but it's not until you read the fine print that you discover they're just offering "resurrection entertainment" and don't, in fact, even possess any of the unholy tomes. Also ask to see clients they've snatched away from death. If they're reputable, they'll be eager; if not, they'll do everything in their power to keep you from finding out they've reanimated almost no one or failed to revive them fully intact (obvious blemishes of decay, insane from realizing they are essentially Frankenstein for real, etc.).

Grief Journal Prompts

1. You donated $1,000 to Oxfam in your loved one's name only to later discover explicit instructions from them to never contribute to an organization fighting famine, which they characterized as "magnificent" and "just the best." What might you do?

2. Where in your home would you place your loved one's urn? Is that a place of honor or callous indifference?

3. If you were starting a scholarship in memory of your loved one, which criteria would best reflect who they were as a person?
    academic achievement
    erratic vegetarianism
    nominal scoliosis
    excellence as homewrecker
    sex-offender chin

4. Your loved one's bucket list contains nothing but the single ominous entry, "Stop the Omega Project!!!" What are three ways you might stop the Omega Project?

CHAPTER VI

SADNESS OUTRAGEOUSLY SIMPLIFIED: THE SIX TYPES OF GRIEVERS

These days, people love taking quizzes that once and for all reveal to them the truth about something deeply stupid, like which Avenger they are or what color aura they have based on what they like at Taco Bell or what flirting style they employ (Captain America, green, and "sass attack," if you're wondering). While it might seem reckless to apply this treatment to something as delicate and potentially fraught as grief, rest assured that there is genuine science undergirding this chapter's evaluation, though it is too complex to explain here or anywhere else. Just accept that it sees right through you.

This test is the Informal Grief Archetype Assessment (IGAA), which will pigeonhole you into a mourning style as represented by a symbolic character. When you've attained this information, you'll not only understand how and why you grieve but also gain lasting insights into who you are more broadly. More than any mere pregnancy test or cancer screening, the results of this assessment will change your life, and that means forever. This moment is incalculably huge for you. I would urge you to prepare yourself, but you couldn't possibly.

Allow yourself about three minutes to complete the entire test.

INSTRUCTIONS

Choose one answer for each of the following questions. If no answers apply, you may leave the question blank—do so as often as you wish.

1. There's a movie you're looking forward to seeing. But when you arrive, you discover it's sold out. What are you thinking?
   a. "This too shall pass."
   b. "Gosh, I feel worse for everyone else who got turned away."
   c. "I'm getting into that movie, and I don't care if I have to fill the whole lobby with dead ushers."
   d. "I was foolish to think I could distance myself from life's agonies for even two hours."
   e. "Now I need a new dark, air-conditioned place to masturbate."

2. A bare white wall stands before you. What do you do?
   a. Imitate the wall.
   b. Ask around and see if any of your friends needs a bare white wall.
   c. Punch and kick the wall until it tries hiding behind itself.
   d. Lie down and press your back against the wall until you're convinced it's spooning you.
   e. Drill a glory hole, then wait as long as it takes for a new friend to appear.

3. How often are you crying each day?

    a. Will cry someday, when and only when the time is right.

    b. Occasionally but mostly in private, so as not to upset others.

    c. Sorry, not giving goddamn tears the satisfaction.

    d. All day, to the point that pets seem concerned.

    e. Enough to form a generous handful of lubricant.

4. You've been invited to a potluck. What are you bringing?

    a. A flavorless but nutrient-rich porridge.

    b. A potato salad you just know everyone's gonna love.

    c. At least fifteen minutes of continuous violence for anyone who fails to rave about your parmesan puffs.

    d. A sense of futility or maybe something super-easy, like soda.

    e. A casserole dish filled with homemade buffalo semen aphrodisiac.

5. Someone asks, "How are you holding up?" What do you tell them?

    a. "Persevering. I find that sleeping in a bathtub filled with ice and broken glass steels my mind."

    b. "Fine, fine, whatever. But how are *you*?"

    c. "I'm giving you sixty seconds to get out of crossbow range."

    d. "There is nothing left of me to answer that question or to even have heard the question in the first place."

    e. "Last night I experimented anally with two friends, nine strangers, and one acquaintance. Now I have eight friends and four enemies."

6. A powerful genie has one leftover wish after his previous master accidentally wished to be torn apart by lions. He also stipulates you may not wish for your loved one to be brought back to life because he is still just an associate genie without resurrection privileges. What do you wish for?

    a. Wishing accomplishes nothing, only work does.

    b. Thanks, but here's a list of disfigured children who could use a wish even more.

    c. Just give me a thousand arms and a thousand baseball bats, and I'll take it from there.

    d. I would wish for this pain to disappear, but I'll only feel worse when it fails.

    e. I'm wishing for the ability to be as sexually attracted to myself as a stranger might be, so that self-pleasuring has a heightened erotic charge and the very sight of myself naked in the mirror is enough to madly arouse me. This would not preclude me from enjoying sex with others, but it would guarantee me, in essence, a sexual partner at all times for the rest of my life.

7. A telemarketer calls. What do you say to get rid of them?

    a. "I am disconnecting now. Be strong. It is the only way."

    b. "I won't give you my credit card info, but I will wait on the line until you feel good about our conversation being over."

    c. "I'm gonna napalm your calling center. I want you to think I'm bluffing so you'll definitely be there when it happens."

    d. "I want to hang up on you, but isn't there enough abandonment in the world?"

    e. "While you're here, how about I guide you through a prostate massage?"

8. You're back at work after bereavement leave. Which *best* reflects how you're spending most of your time?
    a. Fulfilling assigned duties efficiently and without complaint.
    b. Apologizing to coworkers for inconveniencing them with father's catastrophic cardiac event.
    c. Hurling furniture out office window or just into walls if office is windowless.
    d. PowerPoint presentation with final slide begging for hug.
    e. Constructing G-spot stimulator from items in pen caddy.

9. What part of the house are you?
    a. Storm windows.
    b. Family room.
    c. Gun vault.
    d. Crevice under refrigerator.
    e. Vulva-shaped garage.

10. You enter a bar and spot an attractive person sitting alone. How might you start a conversation?
    a. "Hello. I respect your embrace of fortifying solitude."
    b. "Poor thing. It hurts to be friendless."
    c. "Sorry, I was aiming that beer bottle at a different stranger."
    d. "Would you mind if I burdened you with just the tiniest fraction of my misery?"
    e. "Any interest in ducking into a bathroom stall and enacting an erotic personal trainer/client role-play scenario?"

CALCULATING YOUR SCORE

Review your answers to reveal your grief archetype, and consult the corresponding descriptions that follow. Do not retake the test in hopes of being named a different, cooler archetype. The test will know and self-erase.

If most of your answers were *a*, you identify with the **Stoic Overnight Denny's Waitress.***

If most of your answers were *b*, you identify with the **Teacher Calming Her Students Down After Another Teacher's Nervous Breakdown.**

If most of your answers were *c*, you identify with the **Wrathful Circus Elephant.**

If most of your answers were *d*, you identify with the **Gladiator Who Doesn't Really Leave the House Anymore.**

If most of your answers were *e*, you identify with the **Dildo Weathervane.**

If you did not answer a majority of the questions, you identify with the **Faceless Jack-O'-Lantern.**

---

* Sincerity Corner: I think I do too.

THE ARCHETYPES

The Stoic Overnight Denny's Waitress

The Stoic Overnight Denny's Waitress has seen some shit—literally, human, and not in the restroom. It's just part of her burden, along with checking an immobile homeless person in the corner booth for a pulse and serving piled-high Lumberjack Slams to drunk frat boys who she knows by now have zero intention of tipping. Her motto, like yours, is: "Just get through this, baby." It's as basic as withstanding and moving on. Of course, your burden is the loss of a loved one and not the ramifications of coming between a customer and her vicious pimp named Rolo, but you both cope with straight-ahead grit. You're not exactly running from your pain. Like the Stoic Overnight Denny's Waitress, you allow yourself moments of total disconsolation—you've both cried in your car—but you can only handle your feelings one small piece at a time. And then it's back to work for both of you, though only one of you is going to be calling the cops on someone who stuffed a napkin dispenser down his pants and then jumped through the front window.

The Teacher Calming Her Students Down After Another Teacher's Nervous Breakdown

Although she is privately deeply worried about her longtime colleague, the Teacher Calming Her Students Down After Another Teacher's Nervous Breakdown wants the bus full of third graders to know that Mr. Eckert was just exhausted when he shrieked, "I'm gonna blow my fucking brains out!" on the Museum of Natural History field trip. Tending to others in a difficult moment is her sole focus, as is the case for you, despite what you're struggling with inside. For twelve years, the Teacher Calming Her Students Down After Another Teacher's Nervous Breakdown worked closely enough with Mr. Eckert to call him a good friend and never expected him to fall to the ground in front of the totem pole exhibit and whimper, "I can't, I can't, I can't," over and over. But, like you, she is preoccupied with consoling those who might be more vulnerable in this sad, chaotic moment, even to her own detriment. All the energy she and you expend to help others is energy you're both not using to process your own shock and trauma. Maybe you both don't put as much time into healing yourself as you should because you don't realize other people are often stronger than you think—as it turned out, some of the kids were far less shaken than the Teacher Calming Her Students Down After Another Teacher's Nervous Breakdown thought they would be, and still others knew Mr. Eckert was getting divorced and that it was only a matter of time before he went nuts in front of everyone.

The Wrathful Circus Elephant

One minute she was at her usual watering hole on the Tanzanian grasslands, and the next she was dazed and en route—in a not-so-glorified crate—to a circus, where for three years she has worn a tiara and balanced unnaturally on a ball thousands of miles from her babies. You can relate to the Wrathful Circus Elephant's feelings of injustice, of losing something precious suddenly and cruelly. The Wrathful Circus Elephant is mad as hell and will never, ever get into pyramid formation again, preferring instead to give going berserk a try and seeing what her feet can do to a ringmaster's skeleton. Wow, quite a lot, actually! You might be lashing out too, maybe in all directions, in hopes retribution will heal you, even if you're less sure than the Wrathful Circus Elephant of who exactly has wronged you and how. The rampage ends when the Wrathful Circus Elephant is shot in front of hundreds of horrified audience members who are far more shocked by her death than her original torture. Of course, no one's going to shoot you (probably), so you'll have to decide on your own when you're ready to stop hurting others and yourself—but if you unleash some carnage at a circus before you do, you'll have the gratitude of at least one very pissed-off elephant.

The Gladiator Who Doesn't Really Leave the House Anymore

The Gladiator Who Doesn't Really Leave the House Anymore is barely around in the gore-soaked pits these days, and when he does make that rare appearance, he slaughters his opponent and then heads straight home to sob under the covers. Like him, you're too consumed with your inner pain to be out and about unless you absolutely have to, especially since you know you're not yet in a place where you can keep it together—the Gladiator Who Doesn't Really Leave the House Anymore has already risked being burned alive by asking mighty Caesar for a Kleenex. So you're both rarely seen these days because your sadness is just too much, too easily triggered, and you wonder if you'll ever find your way back. And that's OK for now. You both have warriors within you, though with the Gladiator Who Doesn't Really Leave the House Anymore it's not just a forced metaphor, and the time will come when the two of you feel safe to truly reemerge. Gradually, the Gladiator Who Doesn't Really Leave the House Anymore will take pleasure once again in the bloodthirsty howls of the throngs in the colosseum stands, and you'll get back to whatever you were doing that wasn't nearly as cool as fighting with a net and a trident.

The Dildo Weathervane

Beginning as a fixture on the roofs of homes in Colonial America and continuing into the nineteenth century, the Dildo Weathervane used a long, realistically textured dong as an indicator to determine the direction from which the wind was blowing. Like the Dildo Weathervane, you've been in a state of constant arousal, not because you were forged that way by a blacksmith but because your loved one's passing has left you with surplus anxiety that you're struggling to exhaust, as well as a need for extra intimacy. There is no point in the sky that the Dildo Weathervane will not swivel its shaft toward, just as you seek out erotic release anywhere you can find it. The Dildo Weathervane began to be phased out in the 1870s, though a number of intact specimens remain in their original locations atop Boston's Old North Church, Monticello, and several farmhouses among the Pennsylvania Dutch. As time passes and you come to terms with the death of your loved one, your own out-of-control libido will diminish but, like the Dildo Weathervane itself, still make a startling occasional appearance at a neighbor's yard sale.

The Faceless Jack-O'-Lantern

The Faceless Jack-O'-Lantern is *not* a regular pumpkin, though it presents *exactly* like a regular pumpkin. It is, in fact, a jack-o'-lantern, but one deliberately disengaged from its own circumstances. Likewise, you exhibit a dissociation from your grief, unable to put your finger on how to encounter it, so you stand on the sidelines and externalize it out of existence. You, like the Faceless Jack-O'-Lantern, are untouched. Of course, the Faceless Jack-O'-Lantern knows what it actually is, deep down, but is unhappy about it and simply refuses to acknowledge the crooked eyeholes a nine-year-old fucked up or the sloppy mouth which looks like it was caved in by a hoof—the Faceless Jack-O'-Lantern really liked the way things were back in the patch. So did you, and you're not ready to acknowledge you've left just yet. And you have time. The Faceless Jack-O'-Lantern, on the other hand, has until November 1, when it gets tossed into a garbage truck.

Grief Journal Prompts

1. Write nonstop, without editing, for five straight minutes on how the assessment above compares with the most recent version of the Minnesota Multiphasic Personality Inventory (MMPI-2-RF) in terms of structure, validity, and internal consistency. What insights emerged from your journaling?

2. Was the Informal Grief Archetype Assessment sufficiently reductive? How else could it have dumbed down the spectrum of human emotion?

3. Are you surprised by your results? If so, how would you justify that lack of self-awareness in front of a judge? If it helps, draw the judge.

4. If you could create an all-new grief archetype, what would it be? Alternately, the Snowman Who Knows It Can Never Participate in a Hot Dog Eating Contest got cut. Would you like to do something with that?

DON'T WORRY, YOU'LL DIE TOO

It's a bummer when something tragic gets passed down generation after generation. Maybe it's poverty in a society with no opportunity for advancement or an unfortunate recessive gene resulting in a tentacle or two. But even if you're abundantly blessed and the worst thing you inherit from your forebears is almost inconsiderate sex appeal, you will follow in their footsteps in one crucially icky way. You're going to die. You probably knew that, of course, because I mentioned it earlier in the book. I certainly hope you didn't think that death would steer clear of you like the science teacher who knows a particular student always has the right answer and wants to give the other dolts in class a chance. Because when that teacher has had enough of the dumdums who have no future, or at least shouldn't have one, when the ignorance is just too much to bear, he or she will always swing around to that nerd who chirps, "Photosynthesis!" right on cue. In other words, teachers and death eventually call on us all.

And when a loved one dies, we not only mourn their passing but often get around to pondering our own. Because death got close, in real life. Not so close that it can tap a bony finger on our shoulder or even close enough to annoyingly blow leaves from its lawn onto our property. But it feels at least local now, like it roots for the same football team we do and sees the same personal injury attorney ads on TV. It's the single inevitability in our lives—not even our birth *had* to happen—and now we have to sit with the fact that our turn really, really is coming. Really.

Really.

All the questions we might've pondered in the wake of our loved one's death—"What was their experience like?"; "Did it hurt?"; "Did their soul depart for the afterlife, or is it still trapped in their hospital room like a moth?"—blow back in our faces. There's a new urgency for answers but also a new frustration that such urgency isn't suddenly making the unknown known. I mean, if you're very religious, it's all mapped out in terms of what death is like, where you're headed afterward, and who you might expect to be reunited with/eternally ripped to shreds by. But most of us take our questions to the grave.

Those questions also include not just what will happen in the moment we die and what happens to us once we've delicately been transferred to past tense, but what will happen to the memory of us in the world we leave behind: who will grieve for us? You were so moved by the passing of someone that you went out and bought the powerful resource you're currently reading. But will others buy it because of what you meant to *them*? Sure, if you died today, you might expect reasonable attendance at your funeral, something between standing room only and enough empty seats that there's no reason the janitor can't start vacuuming in the back. But now that you've lost someone, it's hard not to contemplate whether you've really done all you can to one day earn the tears from those who matter most.

I could tell you to focus on living in the present, controlling what you actually can control, and treating people, even one or two who don't really deserve it, with kindness. And hey, maybe I will, fuck it, enjoy. But if there's anything that reassures me, quite honestly, it's that we are truly in this death thing together. It weirdly makes the world a bit less lonely. All of us—rich or poor; man, woman, or nonbinary; ping-pong players on either side of the table—have the exact same fate. Sure, one day some tech billionaire will announce he's uploaded his consciousness into the body of an intern who had been wondering why he'd been chosen strictly on the basis of good looks, chiseled physique, and high sperm count, and then death itself will become just another indignity for the poor. But for now, we're all here together until we're not here at all. Maybe we can make something out of that.*

Grief Journal Prompt

1. This is the final grief journal prompt. Since continuing without them would be unproductive, how will you now dispose of your journal?

---

* **Sincerity Corner:** Yeah, maybe.

FURTHER
READING

I neglected to mention earlier that I've actually written twenty other books on dying and grief which you can use to supplement the work you're currently being renewed by. (To avoid redundancy, I did not include the publisher in the list below, as all titles were printed by celebrated press Superstar Creative Endeavors, which I've been assured is not a shady vanity outfit, despite charging me fifty dollars per page for "premium word lacquer" and operating out of a storage locker, though never the same one for very long.)

Ten Things about Grief They Don't Teach You at Hamburger University

A Vulnerable Person's Guide to Cults and Militias

Grief Rituals of Our Ancient Ancestors That Were Obviously Dumb Even Then

Remember You Get To Keep the Deposit Even If Everyone at the Bachelorette Party Says You're Too Bloated to Pass For Channing Tatum: Healing Wisdom from a Celebrity Lookalike

"He What?!" Fifty Writers on Finding Out Just Now That a Loved One Has Died

Saying Goodbye the NordicTrack Way

Take Your Pathetic Mewling to God: Helping a Friend through Grief

Yes, You Can Grieve Like a Cajun!

The Weeping Canapé: The Griever's Guide to Starting a Catering Company

Grandpa Is Pure Nonbeing: Teaching Your Child about Oblivion

Everything I Would've Told My Mother Had My Mouth Not Been So Full of Steak Tips

The Page-A-Day Inspiration Calendar with Maybe a Few Repeats Toward the End

"Why Is This Happening, Gaston?" The Complete Directory of Costumed Disney Mascots Secretly Authorized to Talk to You about Death

Lashing Out like the Pros Do

The Sun Will Rise Again: Poems of Hope I Wrote While Waiting to Report the Debit Card I Lost Somewhere between My Home and Aéropostale

500 Sex Positions for Working through Your Father's Absence

Everything's Impermanent, So Why Should My Own Existence Be Any Different?: Conversations with Kids Who Have Eerily Mature Takes on Death

"Butt Torquing" and 101 Other Isometric Eulogy Exercises

The Caterpillar That's No Longer Hungry and Won't Be with Us Much Longer, I'm Afraid

I Thought Everyone Knew How Much Amy Hates Our Troops: Marginalizing Your Siblings While Your Conservative Grandmother's Still Lucid Enough to Change the Will

ABOUT THE AUTHOR

Jason Roeder is a former senior editor and senior writer at *The Onion* as well as a contributor to *The New Yorker* and McSweeney's Internet Tendency. He is the coauthor of the college catalog parody *Welcome to Woodmont*, named one of *Vulture*'s best humor books of 2022, and of the satirical sex manual *Sex: Our Bodies, Our Junk*, which *Publishers Weekly* described in a starred review as a "hilarious and addictive page-turner." He currently lives in Los Angeles and can also be found at jasonroeder.info.